Sports Buildings   A Briefing and Design Guide

SPORTS BUILDINGS

First published in 1986 by the Architectural Press Ltd,
9 Queen Anne's Gate, London SW1H 9BY

BRITISH LIBRARY CATALOGUING IN PUBLICATION DATA

Konya, Allan
Sports buildings. – (A Briefing and design guide)
1. Recreation centres – Great Britain
2. Sports facilities – Great Britain
I. Title   II. Series
725′.8   NA6800

ISBN 0-85139-761-1

Typeset by Crawley Composition Ltd, Crawley
Printed and bound in Great Britain by Biddles Ltd,
Guildford and King's Lynn

Acknowledgements

The development of this rather ambitious series of books – first suggested by Maritz Vandenberg (then the Commissioning Editor for Architectural Press Books) in April 1979 – has been a long and tiring process and would not have reached its present stage without the continuous support and encouragement given by Maritz and his colleagues throughout these years.

Although inspired by the series of Briefing and Design Guides which appeared in *The Architects' Journal* during the 1960s, the format has been revised and the contents completely rewritten and updated. The author is indebted to a number of people for their help, in particular: Mike Jenks of The Department of Architecture at Oxford Polytechnic, and Dr Frank Duffy of DEGW (Architects and Space Planners) for reading and re-reading parts of the manuscript, for offering invaluable criticism and advice, and for providing useful reference material; Professor Henry Sanoff (author of Methods of Architectural Programming) for reading the introduction and making suggestions for improvements; Professors Alewyn Burger and Dieter Holm for their help with defining the problem at the start of the project; *The Architects' Journal* for permission to reproduce photographs in Appendix 3; and last but not least, Dorothy Pontin and her assistants in The Architectural Press Library for finding so much of the reference material that was needed.

Thanks must go to a number of specialist manufacturers of sports and recreation equipment who generously provided information and photographs, and to the following institutions for their assistance: The Sports Council, The Institute of Baths and Recreation Management, The Institute of Leisure and Amenity Management, The Royal Institute of Chartered Surveyors, The British Institute of Interior Design and The Landscape Institute.

Contents

Inception and initial brief

Feasibility

Detailed brief

Outline proposals/scheme design

Appendices

Introduction

1.   Who is this book for?

The main purpose of these *Briefing and Design Guides* is to provide all those involved in the initial stages of the building process – clients, users and members of the design team – with a set of tools. These tools, or resources, will help them communicate more effectively so that they are able to work together to develop rich design briefs which will, it is hoped, culminate in the best solutions to their particular problems.

There are a few points to be stressed. First, for every building within each major type covered by this series there is a wide range of variables: the building may be large or small, simple or complex; the client may be a public body, a large private organisation or a small firm, a family or an individual; those involved may be experienced or inexperienced in building; the design team may be big or small, may or may not have experience with the relevant building type; and every team will have its individual method of working. It is impossible to cover all the likely combinations and to provide an ideal set of guidelines for all clients, users and designers in all situations. There will obviously, therefore, tend to be a bias in these *Guides* towards a particular briefing context that is not the most simple nor the most complex, but rather a fairly uncomplicated middle range. In spite of this it should be possible to use each *Guide*, if one realises and accepts its limitations, as a basic tool not only for the simplest but also for the most complex of projects.

Secondly, there is no one way of approaching the design process – and this is also true of briefing. Procedures will vary, for example, between those used by and for different types of client, and by and for the public and private sectors. Although the contents of each *Guide* are organised and presented in a specific linear sequence, as demonstrated in Fig. 0.1, they should not be seen or used as a rigid set of sequential instructions but rather as a loose framework, or flexible tool, which can be adapted to suit individual requirements.

Thirdly, the guidance contained in these books is intended for the main

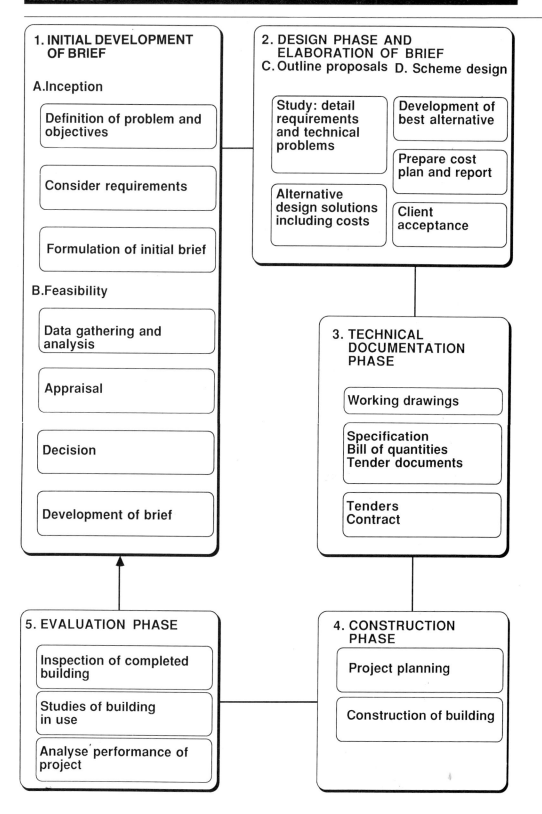

1. INITIAL DEVELOPMENT OF BRIEF

A. Inception

Definition of problem and objectives

Consider requirements

Formulation of initial brief

B. Feasibility

Data gathering and analysis

Appraisal

Decision

Development of brief

2. DESIGN PHASE AND ELABORATION OF BRIEF
C. Outline proposals D. Scheme design

Study: detail requirements and technical problems

Alternative design solutions including costs

Development of best alternative

Prepare cost plan and report

Client acceptance

3. TECHNICAL DOCUMENTATION PHASE

Working drawings

Specification
Bill of quantities
Tender documents

Tenders
Contract

5. EVALUATION PHASE

Inspection of completed building

Studies of building in use

Analyse performance of project

4. CONSTRUCTION PHASE

Project planning

Construction of building

Fig. 0.1 *The main phases and steps of the complete briefing and design process. This book is specifically concerned with phases 1 and 2. (Based on stages A to D of 'Plan of Work'; see Appendix A.1.a.)*

participants in the process of briefing and design, but it is not always possible to distinguish clearly between that which is, for example, specifically the role of the client, and that which is the responsibility of others. It is not advisable to generalise about who should undertake each and every task: this is something to be determined by those involved in each individual project. Wherever possible, however, an indication is given of who is most likely to be responsible.

2. What is design?

The design of buildings is, at its simplest, the creative development of an idea – in three-dimensional form – to solve a specific problem. This problem-solving activity is called the 'design process'. This term is generally used to describe everything that happens from the time a problem is first outlined to the finalised design. The methods used can range from those based on intuition and experience on the one hand, to extremely formal and inflexible logical or mathematical approaches on the other. Whether consciously applied or not, virtually all of the procedures will include the following actions in one form or another:

— recognition and definition of the problem and objectives and consideration of the component sub-problems.
— observation and collection of data relevant to the problem.
— analysis of requirements and data collected.
— development of alternative ideas and solutions. Design can never produce the one correct answer, and from the innumerable possibilities those that seem most suitable for the specific problem will be sought.
— synthesis, or the putting together of ideas to form complete designs.
— evaluation, or the testing of alternative designs against requirements, and optimisation.

The process is not a simple linear sequence of logical steps leading neatly from one phase to another – of finding the right answer at each step or phase before progressing to the next – but rather a series of actions comprising steps grouped for convenience into phases, some or all of which may occur simultaneously. As new information becomes available ideas that seemed perfectly adequate at an earlier step or phase may have to be changed. Indeed, the complete cycle of actions may have to be reconsidered several times.

3. The importance of the brief

In a world of increasing complexity and rapid technological change, the whole process of design and building has become ever more difficult. There has been an increase not only in the number of different types of buildings needed, but also in the size and complexity of projects. The number of alternatives has also increased: more feasible solutions, more materials, systems and technologies available, more experts and specialists, and a greater number of schools of thought than in the past. In addition, there are countless other problems to be contended with: bureaucracy, controls, regulations and standards; new imperatives such as energy conservation and changing social needs; the explosion of information; economic constraints and a growing demand for guaranteed performance-in-use. Also, as the process becomes more involved and susceptible to delays, time becomes a scarcer commodity and developments are expected much faster.

The increasingly complex operations to be performed, the mass of information to be collected, the involvement of many people who have contributions to make, and the number of decisions to be taken in the design of even the simplest of buildings, have all made it more and more difficult to rely on intuition and experience alone. As a result thorough briefing has, in recent years, rightly come to be seen as an integral part of the design process.

4.   How to use this book

Each *Guide* covers a major building type. Section 1 is relevant to all projects: it provides an outline description of the briefing process and the main participants and gives detailed guidelines for the initial procedure that is basic to any project. It stands as a checklist for the architect, as well as supplying clients with a framework within which to consider their requirements.

The main body of the text is contained in Section 2. This is specific to the building type and includes aids to concept-selection and basic design information. It is divided into five parts: introduction, inception, feasibility, detailed brief and design. The text is in the form of instructions and checklists with comprehensive source and detail information, and is backed up by the appendices. The first three parts of Section 2 are for all concerned with the briefing/design process. The last two parts are intended mainly for the design team but can usefully be referred to by clients and users so that they are aware of the type of information required by the design team for the later design stages.

SECTION ONE
GENERAL

Introduction

1.1 Buildings

Buildings represent, amongst other things, energy, labour and materials. These either cannot be replaced or can only be replaced at great cost. The severe economic recession, the energy crisis and an awareness that resources are finite have led to the realisation that existing buildings are a valuable commodity to be conserved, regardless of their historic or architectural merits, and in addition, that new buildings must be designed and built to last.

Building development today is increasingly concerned with the recycling of space in one way or another. This may be done by:

— extension or addition to a structure owned by the client to provide more space or new facilities.

— alteration of, or modification to, existing premises, which does not lead to a change of use.

— maintenance or refurbishment of an existing structure to improve its appearance and prolong its life.

— conversion of existing premises involving a change of use, for example, from a warehouse to offices or an hotel.

Conversion and rehabilitation are important not only from the point of view of physical resources, but also as a means of revitalising older, densely built, run-down inner-city areas.

In the case of new work and of many conversion or extension projects, a major goal is to provide a building of 'long life, low energy usage and loose fit' – in other words, to reduce capital turnover by making it continually viable with low fuel and maintenance costs as well as easily adaptable to changing use. On the point of changing use: although it is important to identify and design for the specific users, there is an increasing emphasis on flexibility so that the building created will be adaptable to the extent of being able to accommodate changes in activities and requirements during a lifespan of 50 years or more.

1.2   Design and construction methods

There are two basic approaches, each with variations, which a client can adopt for the design and construction of new building work, and an early decision has to be taken on which general method will be most appropriate for the project.

One option is to employ independent consultants for the design and then, at a later stage, a contractor to build the project. This method is used for many projects of all types and sizes undertaken by private clients, and has several advantages. For example, it allows the freedom to choose a briefing and design team most suited to one's specific needs from the large variety of consultant firms. It also allows the freedom to obtain competitive tenders for the construction, based on the same drawings and specifications, although it is possible for the design team to negotiate with a single contractor.

The other option is to employ a single firm for both the design and the construction of the project, a method also referred to as a 'package deal' or a 'turn-key' operation. There are a variety of construction companies offering this type of integrated service. Some supply standard buildings only, some undertake one-off projects, some do both; some specialise in building types, for example, warehouses, factories, offices, hotels, schools or housing; some produce building systems which they use in their projects; some specialise in simple single-storey structures, while others undertake complex and multi-storey projects. These companies employ their own professional staff, either in-house or outside consultants, who develop the brief and design for specific projects. Although it is possible to approach different companies and have each submit a proposal, it can be difficult to compare prices as they will not be based on identical designs and specifications. The client may, furthermore, have to bear the costs of the proposals submitted by the unsuccessful firms. While this method may save time and/or money on certain types of projects, a disadvantage can be the lack of advice from the consultants of one's own choice.

Which of the two basic methods is used will depend largely on the nature of the problem, the type, size and complexity of the proposed project, as well as the time available for its completion. It is ultimately up to the client and his initial advisers to investigate alternatives and make sure that participants, whether independent consultants or design/construct firms, are carefully selected.

1.3   The brief and the briefing process

Once the client has decided to investigate the possibility of altering, extending or converting an existing building, or erecting a new one, the first phase of the proposed project begins. This is the development of the brief through the process of briefing.

A brief is usually a document which can vary considerably in length, content and form depending upon the nature and complexity of the project. It is, amongst other things, a recorded statement of intent and a set of criteria and instructions, including proposals by the design team approved by the client. It is influenced by and derived from the consideration of many factors such as budget, climate, site, legal constraints, user requirements, the way things are used and change through time, and the trade-off between cost and feasibility. It states a set of desired

Fig. 1.1 *Different forms of brief: this may be either one of the four shown or a combination of them (e.g. 1 and 4), and typical organisation of contents.*

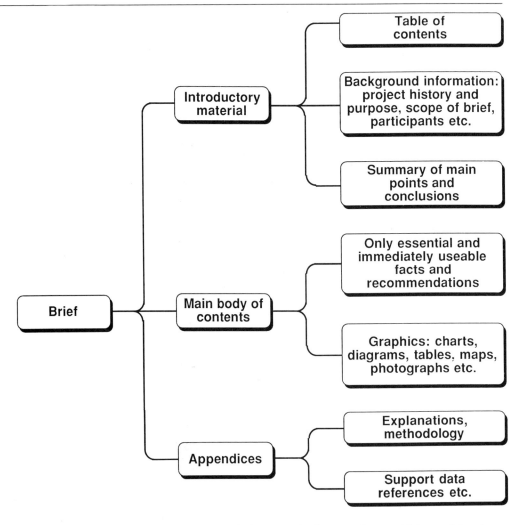

conditions and it is a way of defining, ordering and specifying objectives, requirements and intentions systematically, as well as outlining the methods for achieving them.

Rather than being an end in itself, the brief is a tool that can help those involved to achieve certain desirable ends. It can be used in different ways depending on the problem. For example, a preliminary brief can assist the client to select the right designers and other specialist advisers; a more developed brief (interim or final) may be used as a competition document or a contractual document forming part of a legal agreement between the client and other parties. Although the ultimate goal is usually to provide the specific information and recommendations that are needed and can be used for designing the building, the brief is also used to determine feasibility and may lead to the abandonment of the project.

Starting with a preliminary statement prepared by the client (possibly with professional help), the brief is developed and constantly refined through a process of communication, investigation, analysis and evaluation. The process of briefing

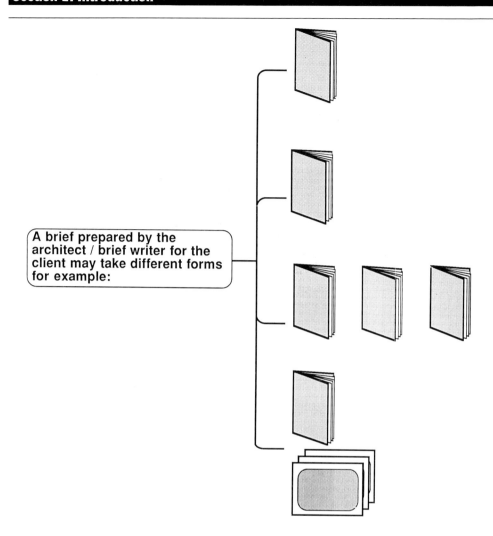

A brief prepared by the architect / brief writer for the client may take different forms for example:

1. *A short preliminary report.*

2. *A comprehensive document covering all aspects of the building design.*

3. *A series of reports relating definable issues or phased accomplishments.*

4. *A special purpose report covering a specific aspect such as energy conservation or site analysis/survey. This may also take the form of an audiovisual presentation.*

is, in other words, one of dialogue between all concerned; a process of finding as well as solving problems; of determining and defining objectives, constraints, resources, subjective and objective criteria; of determining and exploring what is appropriate and possible, evaluating proposals and making recommendations. Briefing is often controversial since, while technical requirements can usually be quantified, this is often not possible with other more abstract criteria. It should therefore be a process of debate and a means of decision-making, encouraging participation by, and feedback from, all the participants.

The brief, therefore, changes and grows continuously as the design proceeds. The design solution evolves from the brief and can, in turn, clarify and expand it through early design work which helps to identify problems, objectives and criteria. When it is realised in the completed project, it also has a role in post-construction evaluation. After a certain point in the design process, which will vary from project to project, major changes to the brief can lead to abortive work and have cost implications for the client or the design team.

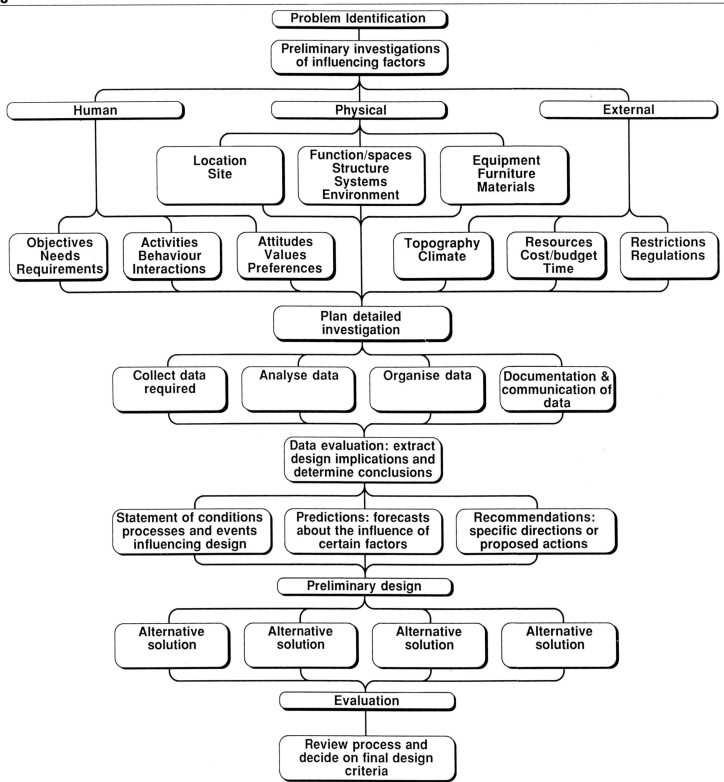

Although, as has already been stressed, there is no one way of approaching briefing, it always forms the foundation of the design process and constitutes an integral part of this process. For these reasons and because there are usually so many factors and variables involved in the design of even the simplest building, it is important that the brief be objectively, imaginatively and comprehensively developed whatever the method used.

1.4   The main participants

The main groups involved in the process of briefing and design are the client, the users, the professional brief writer and the design team.

The client

The client is the person or organisation initiating and paying for the project. There are many different types of client ranging from private individuals to complex private and public organisations. Not only is the nature of each type different but so also are their needs, objectives, values, priorities, resources and restraints. Some build for their own use; others are providers of space rather than users of the building; yet others act for and on behalf of the actual users; for some, building is a commercial venture, while for others the basic motive may, for example, have to do with welfare, education or culture.

While clients in the public sector are controlled by predetermined rules and procedures affecting organisation, approval, financing and time-scale, private clients have relative freedom. Client responsibilities also tend to differ. In the public sector, the client departments are very often responsible not only for initiating the project, selecting the site, instructing the consultants and monitoring progress, but also for gathering and co-ordinating information from various departments, producing the initial brief and preparing the documents required for outline planning applications, loan sanctions, and so on.

Private clients, on the other hand, often leave some of these responsibilities, for example, the gathering and organisation of basic data, and preparation of an initial (or preliminary) brief, to the architect. Alternatively they may appoint a professional brief writer to assist them. At an early stage the client must determine the extent of his personal involvement which should, at the very least, be sufficient to ensure that responsibilities delegated to others are being adequately discharged.

It is not difficult for individual clients or small organisations to have a simple, ideally single, line of contact between themselves and the other participants. However, the more complex the client body – the greater the number of people, departments and sections involved, and the greater the levels of hierarchy – the more difficult it becomes to determine just who is the client. It follows that in this case it is important for the roles and responsibilities of all those involved, in management, professional and advisory capacities, and for the channels of communication (particularly on a day-to-day basis) to be clearly defined to avoid delays and confusion.

Fig. 1.2 *Although the briefing process can be approached in different ways, the flow chart at left outlines the common activities involved in developing the required information.*

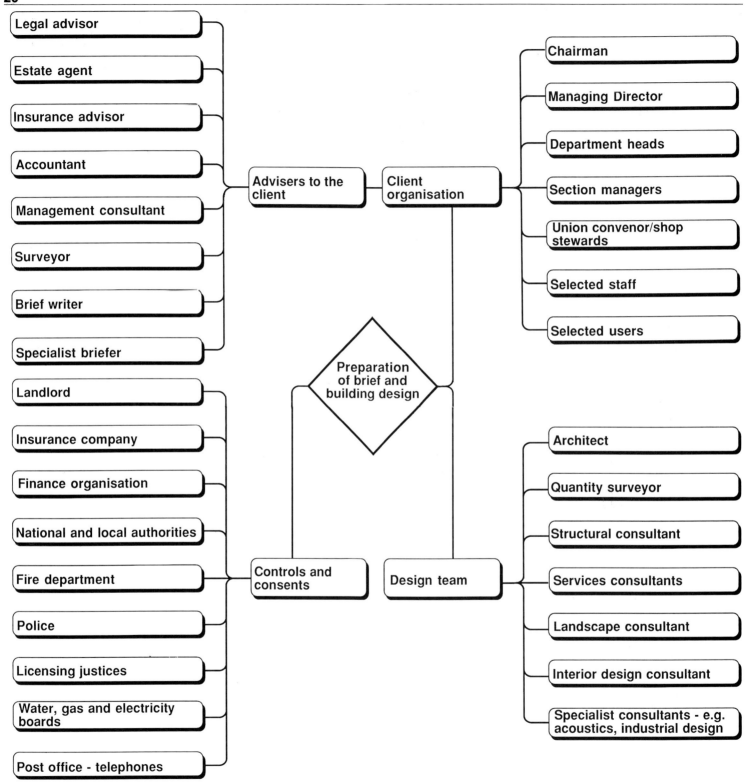

- Legal advisor
- Estate agent
- Insurance advisor
- Accountant
- Management consultant
- Surveyor
- Brief writer
- Specialist briefer

Advisers to the client

- Landlord
- Insurance company
- Finance organisation
- National and local authorities
- Fire department
- Police
- Licensing justices
- Water, gas and electricity boards
- Post office - telephones

Controls and consents

Preparation of brief and building design

Client organisation

- Chairman
- Managing Director
- Department heads
- Section managers
- Union convenor/shop stewards
- Selected staff
- Selected users

Design team

- Architect
- Quantity surveyor
- Structural consultant
- Services consultants
- Landscape consultant
- Interior design consultant
- Specialist consultants - e.g. acoustics, industrial design

The users

The users are those who will actually use the building: they may live, work, play or relax in it; they may be permanent inhabitants or employees who use it daily, or members of the general public who visit it regularly or occasionally. Clients and users are very often different bodies: public authorities and speculative developers are examples of clients who, together with their professional consultants, brief and design on behalf of the eventual users. As a result, few users have the opportunity of influencing the original design, and all too often their requirements and likely use of the spaces are based on assumptions.

In many building types there is the problem of different kinds of users. In hospitals, for example, nurses, doctors, patients and visitors are all users. They may have different or even conflicting requirements. The various categories of user must be identified at an early stage as it is important to understand the implications of their requirements, and to be responsive to them. How this is done will depend on circumstances and vary from project to project. One or more of the following methods may be used:

— direct involvement and participation: permanent staff or regular users may be represented or consulted through unions, local organisations and pressure groups. This encourages an active role in the process by helping to define problems and objectives, to generate concepts and evaluate alternatives. In some instances this might be essential, while in others it might hinder the process or be impossible.

— social science and other user studies: a helpful source of data, but care should be taken because such studies may be generalised and in the planning of a building specific requirements are necessary. On the other hand it must also be borne in mind that the very specific data which is often provided in these studies may not necessarily be relevant to any one particular problem. If studies are to be carried out specifically for a project by surveys, interviews, questionnaires or observation, for example, the designers' limitations must be taken into account and collaboration with suitable consultants from the field of human sciences should be considered.

— surveys of similar building types in use to provide feedback on user requirements. Many of the building studies published in architectural journals tend to concentrate on visual aesthetics and technical aspects, lacking sufficient information on actual usage. If private surveys are undertaken, the method of study and appraisal should place emphasis on evidence from various users: on the deficiencies and advantages they find while living, working, playing or relaxing in the building in question.

The professional brief writer

The professional brief writer specialises in helping clients determine and describe their building needs. This person is, generally speaking, qualified not only to carry out analytical, objective, unbiased and creative studies of the clients' and users' needs, but also to understand their implications for design. He may be:

— a member of the client organisation.

Fig. 1.3 *People who may be involved in the briefing and design process. Just who will participate will depend, amongst other things, on the size of the client organisation and on the type and complexity of the project.*

— an architect who provides a briefing service either separately or as part of design services (see also Appendix A.4).

— a professional brief writer, who may or may not be an architect, but who specialises in the process of briefing and the preparation of briefs.

— a briefing specialist who provides a service for a particular building type.

The professional brief writer may only be involved with preparing an initial policy-briefing document or may be retained, with the approval of the architect and other members of the design team, to help develop a detailed brief, and possibly to help evaluate plans and proposals, as the work progresses.

The design team

The design team is made up of the architect together with various other appointed consultants each of whom specialise in one aspect of the design process. The team may include a quantity surveyor, structural, electrical and mechanical engineers, an interior designer, a landscape architect, as well as other specialists from various disciplines, possibly used on a short-term or *ad hoc* basis as dictated by the project. The responsibilities of this group include advising the client and users of the options available to them, assisting with the development of the brief, and carrying out the actual designing and managing activities.

In very large or very complex projects it may be necessary to include an experienced project manager or project controller who would be responsible for the overall co-ordination and monitoring of the total project from inception to completion. This person may be an architect, surveyor or engineer specialising exclusively in this service, and usually also acts as the liaison officer between all the parties involved.

All these consultants are generally in private practices, and although some large consultant firms may include a variety of specialists under one roof they are certain to need outside help on occasion. The same is true of the public sector and large private client organisations that have their own design offices.

1.5 Approvals

Another group of people who, although not directly involved in the briefing and design process, exert an important influence on all phases of the work, are the representatives of the various public authorities responsible for applying the appropriate legislation and regulations. There is a vast amount which governs new building work and involves discussion with and formal application to various public authorities. For example:

— planning applications – for new developments, changes of use and certain extensions – to the appropriate local planning authority. These are usually in two stages: the first is an 'outline' application giving information on the general intention; the second is a 'full' application accompanied by drawings illustrating the scheme in detail.

— application to the local authority responsible for administering the Building Regulations. Detailed drawings, specifications and structural calculations must be submitted and approval obtained before any construction work begins.

— the local fire authority must inspect and approve premises before issuing a fire certificate; the local health officer and the district surveyor will need to be consulted on requirements for fire precautions, lighting, ventilation and the provision of sanitary conveniences.

— other individuals or organisations may have to be consulted or give their approval: for example, the local gas, electricity, water and telephone authorities; the landlord or lessor; the insurance company; owners of adjoining properties.

It will be evident from this introduction that the statutory implications of embarking on new building work can be daunting to say the least. The exercise of attending to the requirements is a time-consuming and often a frustrating one, usually taken care of by the architect and other members of the design team. However, some applications, such as special licences, have to be attended to by the client himself, possibly with legal help.

Inception and the preliminary brief

The aim of this phase is to prepare a general outline of requirements and to plan future action. The procedure is a sequence of actions, listed below, which, generally speaking, is standard (in basics only) for all projects irrespective of building type. These steps are supplementary to those given under Section 2, 'Inception and initial brief', and should be used in conjunction with them.

The client must take certain action, possibly with professional help, before any real work on the brief commences. The problem must be defined: the questions who? what? why? where? when? and how? must be considered.

1.6   Client to define problem

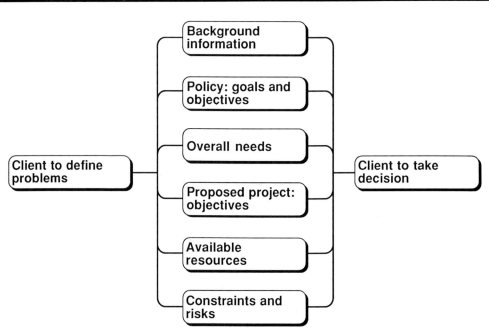

Background information

Describe the client enterprise/body as fully as possible, for example:
— function or purpose for existence, and activities.
— philosophy and history.
— structure and method of operation.
— characteristics: whether conservative or experimental, formal or informal.
— existing facilities with information on problems.

Members of the client body (for example, management, department heads, key staff) should be brought in and encouraged to assist with the various aspects of problem definition and formulation of objectives.

Although it may not be appropriate to set up a briefing and design team at this stage, preliminary general advice may be needed on various aspects such as legal, estate, management and financial which will vary with such factors as the experience of the client and the size and complexity of the proposed project.

Policy: goals and objectives

Determine what the aims and policies are for future growth and change in terms of:
— overall functions to be fulfilled.
— size, achievement, performance, organisation.
— short (2-year), medium (5-year) and long (10-year-plus) term.

Consider:
— why these objectives are important. What the alternatives are. Who will benefit from the achievement of the objectives.
— other parties involved (for example, user groups) who may have different or conflicting objectives.
— what the overriding priorities are.

Overall needs

Estimate present and future overall needs in terms of:
— number and type of staff and/or users.
— activities and equipment to be housed.

Estimate need for additional building space over short (2-year), medium (5-year) and long (10-year-plus) term.

Proposed project: objectives

Formulate in general terms (not detail) objectives for, and broad scope of, proposed project: What is required of it? What will it include and exclude? What are the priorities?

Consider:
— location, site, relationship with other buildings, landscaping.
— size of proposed building: number of people, type of process and equipment, activities it must accommodate. What floor area is required?
— special spaces or facilities required and special equipment to be housed.
— internal environment: ventilation, lighting, heating and services.
— energy use/conservation.
— maintenance.
— lifespan and flexibility: probable changes of use over time.

At this stage all that it requires are broad guidelines rather than rigid details; there must be flexibility for continual development and change – for additions, omissions and revisions.

To generate and develop ideas, and establish priorities, techniques such as brainstorming may be useful. See Appendix A.5 for a summary of these and references to useful sources of more detailed information.

Fig. 1.4 *Defining and ranking objectives.*

1 = objective in row is preferred to objective in column

0 = objective in column is preferred to objective in row

It is impossible to start the process of briefing and design without first defining objectives which are, because of the nature of the problem, difficult to separate from the ways of achieving them. One way of exploring and clarifying objectives is to construct an objective 'tree'. Start by listing the known objectives. For example, when considering the design of fire protection for a building the broad goals might be to:

— reduce likelihood of death or injury to occupants and users.

— protect the building fabric.

— protect the contents.

Each of these can be expanded into sub-objectives that can be further sub-divided:

The first basic objective, to reduce likelihood of death and injury, can be analysed in the same way. The objective 'tree' itself does not provide any answers and these are most likely to come as a result of working through the process itself: as a result of asking oneself the questions what? why? how? The exercise should provide a starting-point for discussion that will help to identify which objectives really are essential, which are compatible with each other, and how each relates to the resources available.

Once objectives are identified a matrix can be used to help determine objectives. The value of this method becomes more apparent when there is a large list of objectives to consider making it more difficult to rank them intuitively. One disadvantage is that comparison by pairs can result in illogical responses, for example, choosing B over A, A over C and then C over B. If such a matrix is filled in by a number of people the results should be randomly checked for such responses to ensure that they are valid.

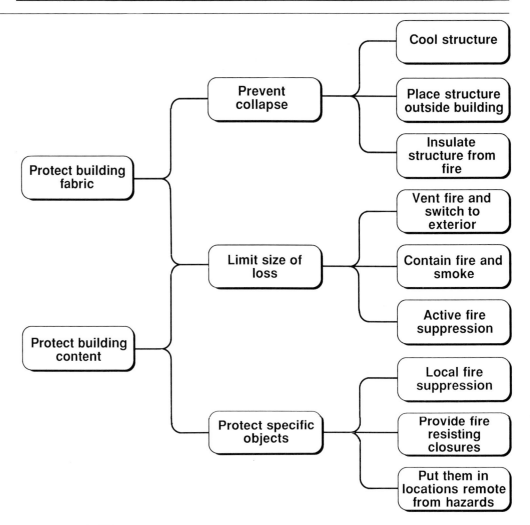

Objective	A	B	C	D	E	Row totals	Ranking
A		0	0	0	1	1	4
B	1		1	0	1	3	2
C	1	0		0	1	2	3
D	1	1	1		1	4	1
E	0	0	0	0		0	5

—   prestige level externally and internally: appearance, height of building/ spaces, quality of finishes.
—   timing: How important is completion date? How urgent is starting date? Can project be done in phases?
—   cost implications within a time-frame.

Available resources

Estimate your own and all other available present and future resources, for example:
—   own finance, manpower, time, building space and land.
—   access to other finance: share issue, grants and loans.
—   availability of materials, manpower, energy and land.

Constraints and risk

Determine all possible constraints:
—   shortage of resources, for example, finance and time, and/or cost of capital needed.
—   site.
—   legal and consents: special licence required, planning consent.
—   tax implications in terms of time-scale.

Consider various ways of reconciling need and objectives with available resources without undue risk, for example:
—   cash flow and commitment of resources.
—   risk assessment, spread and sharing.

1.7   Decision

In terms of the foregoing consider reasons for and against building:
—   is there really a need or demand for the type of facility under review?
—   relate potential need/demand and stated objectives to resources, constraints and risks: What does one wish to accomplish? Will it be possible to achieve this?

Consider which of the following will be most appropriate:
—   decrease demand or need for building space.
—   rent space.
—   buy building suited to needs.
—   buy and convert building.
—   expand or adapt present accommodation.
—   build new building.

This is a preliminary decision only: it is a decision to proceed to the next stage, that is to invest time and a predetermined sum of money to start the formal process of briefing and design in order to investigate in detail the feasibility of the proposed project.

A decision to go ahead may be the correct one at this stage. The briefing and design process extends over a period of time, however, and as new information becomes available at a later stage it will be necessary to review the decision.

1.8 Initial procedures by client

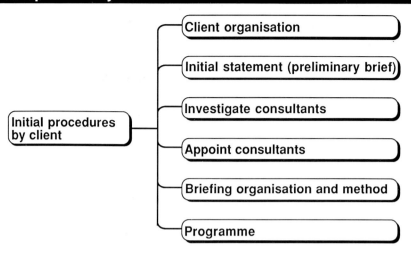

Client organisation
Set up organisation for decision-making and for management of the project from the client side.
Consider the following:
— committee or working party.
— departmental representatives.
— liaison with briefing and design team particularly on a day-to-day basis.
Determine roles and responsibilities of all concerned including who will be responsible for initial statement:
— is there sufficient expertise within the client organisation to do the required work?
— if not, consider appointing a professional brief writer or approaching specialists appropriate to this task.

Initial statement (preliminary brief)

This statement should be based on information and ideas used to arrive at the decision to proceed. It may be prepared by the client, someone within the client organisation or a professional brief writer.
Steps listed under 1.9 can be used as a checklist for the kind of information that should be included.

Prepare a written preliminary document: a statement of aims and requirements including all available relevant information. Describe:
— the nature of the client body and the implications of that fact.
— why a building is needed.
— what objectives should be met by the proposed building, setting out priorities.

Investigate consultants

For summarised guidance on services offered, fees charged etc. by the main groups of consultants see Appendix A.4.
The type and size of project, as well as, amongst other things, the aesthetic qualities envisaged will influence the choice of architect and the decision on what other consultants/specialists are required.

Determine what consultants will be required at this stage and whether they should be appointed for developing the brief only or for briefing and design:
— professional brief writer and/or briefing specialist.
— architect.
— surveyor: for obtaining accurate site information or when adapting/ converting existing building.

—   quantity surveyor: for cost estimates.
—   structural, mechanical and electrical engineers.
—   other specialists: landscape architect, interior designer.

Investigate suitable firms and ascertain position with regard to services provided, fees, contracts etc. Consider, amongst other things:

—   experience of architects and other consultants in dealing with similar building types/projects.
—   personalities: close working relationship and confidence between all concerned is important.

Appoint consultants

Approach selected firms and discuss terms. Appoint the following:

—   architect: to prepare brief only; or for complete project; or something in between.
—   other consultants required now; further appointments may have to be made at a later stage.

Consult architect for his recommendations regarding the most suitable consultants.

Formal agreement should include definitions of limits of responsibility, precise scope of services to be provided, time implications, details of fees and expenses etc. Standard forms may be used; exchange of letters may be adequate.

Briefing organisation and method

Establish formal organisation for briefing and design process: committee, steering group etc. Identify likely participants and define:

—   relationship to client organisation (see p.28).
—   a single client instruction route. This is particularly important if the client is a public authority or a government department, or in the case of a joint use project with more than one client.
—   responsibilities and procedures, for example, administration and control.
—   role to be played in process by users and/or user organisations.

Decide on briefing methods:

—   communication: regular meetings, circulation of documents etc.
—   documentation, for example, recording of data and decisions for easy retrieval and reference.
—   techniques: surveys, use of computer etc.

An outline of some briefing methods and techniques is given in Appendix A.5; for more detailed information see Appendix A.1.a: Jones[1], Palmer[2], Preiser[3] and Sanoff[4].

Fig. 1.5 *A. A simple bar chart showing estimated duration of sequential steps or activities in relation to a time scale. Dependencies between the activities are not indicated in such a chart. This means that should one activity be delayed it is not immediately apparent how this will affect subsequent events. B. A critical path method (CPM) chart in which interconnecting arrows form a network diagram with the time of each activity shown below each arrow (in curved brackets). This is a sophisticated method used for charting time overlaps and activity interdependencies amongst other things, and from which the critical path – the sequence of interdependent activities which establishes the shortest possible time in which a project can be completed – is determined.*

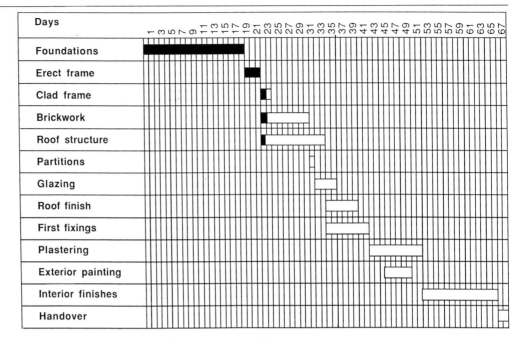

A.

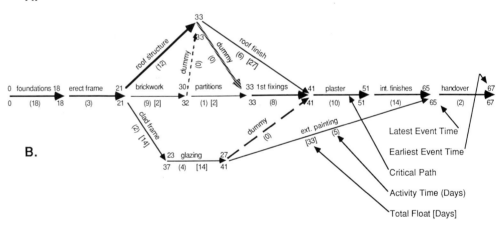

B.

Use Section 2 as a checklist of steps to be taken/tasks to be done. A simple linear sequence will not, however, be suitable for drawing up a programme since there is bound to be overlapping. Techniques are available to help in the preparation of charts that relate overlapping steps to time. See Fig. 1.5.

A quantity surveyor and an accountant will be best suited to give advice on building economics and financial implications. For outline information see Appendix A.4.

Programme

Identify and schedule briefing and design work:
— list tasks to be done and decisions to be made.
— assign responsibilities: who will be involved with each task and when.
— estimate financial and other resources needed.

Determine realistic timetable. Consider:
— key target dates set by external circumstances: expiry of lease on existing premises etc.
— dates for building commencement and completion.
— effect of seasons on building operations.
— scope of project and quality of work required.

— availability of manpower.
— cash flow over time.
— financial implications of timing, for example, income on investment versus interest paid on loan.

1.9 General data and objectives

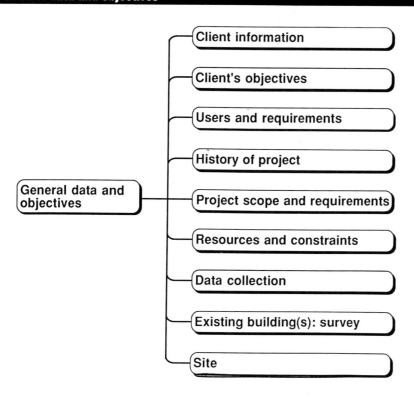

Although addressed to the architect the following should be used by the client, and whoever assists him, as a guideline to the information required in the 'Initial statement' (see p.28). Read together with 2.6.

Client information

Evaluate preliminary client statement. Check that all information on the nature and character of the client enterprise/body is available:
— what they do, how they do it: public authority, joint venture, private concern or other.
— whom they employ or collaborate with.
— involvement with outside services.
— corporate priorities and the likelihood of change.

Client's objectives

Ensure that all information regarding the client's overriding objectives and priorities – both short and long term – is available:
— financial return required or service to the community (social, cultural, educational).
— image to be projected.
— planned or predicted growth and likelihood of change.

Users and requirements

Method(s) used will vary with circumstances and building type. For a broad description of survey methods see Appendix A.5.

Establish who the potential users are if not the client. If possible take steps to contact the different kinds of users. Decide how user requirements are to be communicated/determined, for example:
— direct involvement/consultation: through union or elected representatives.
— and/or through questionnaire/survey.
— and/or through building studies.

History of project

It may be necessary to contact any other architect involved in accordance with RIBA code of conduct.
If possible/relevant go through client records and documents for information directly related to proposed project. Avoid duplicating work already done, for example, data collection.

Check whether any work has previously been undertaken:
— feasibility or other.
— have any other consultants been involved? Has their work been paid for?
— have any decisions already been made?
— has data already been collected?

Project scope and requirements

Who decides what will depend upon circumstances. The architect and/or professional brief writer must, however, ensure that the client and users are aware of the available options, and that the necessary decisions are made and understood by all.
See Appendix A.1.a: Alexander[5] which is a useful tool for all involved in the briefing and design process: a variety of options at various levels/scales are listed and described.

Determine the scope, limitations and basic requirements of the proposed project:
— demand for the type of facility envisaged.
— proposed size; future expansion; phasing? If maximum predicted space is built immediately can present surplus be sub-let?
— degree of flexibility/adaptability required, i.e. the likely use of the building over a period of time.
— character envisaged.
— interface with outside world, for example, free or controlled access.
— requirements for space and equipment; relationships between component parts, individuals etc; standards for accommodation – environmental, finishes etc.
— other criteria, for example, energy conservation.

Resources and constraints

For detailed information on the building regulations in the UK see Appendix A.1.a: Elder[6a]; Speaight[7] is a useful reference covering the law of property and land and building regulations amongst other things.

Ensure that all necessary information on available resources and possible constraints is either included in the initial statement or, alternatively, obtained from the client. Consider particularly:
— budget (cost limit): what is included in the cost of building, equipment and furniture, landscaping, consultants' fees?
— whether the effects of inflation have been taken into account.
— recommended and mandatory standards, statutory requirements, regu-

lations and restrictions affecting the project. Draw up a list for reference purposes.

— other resources that can be used (expertise, manpower) and imposed constraints (cash flow, time limits).

— how the resources and constraints relate to the requirements and objectives.

Data collection

Organise and analyse data presently available. Consider:

— relevance, relationships, priorities.

— what information still needs to be obtained and/or confirmed. For what purpose?

— the form in which it is required, by when it will be needed and who will carry out the various tasks. How will this affect the programme (see p.30)?

— the primary information sources for the different kinds of data needed: client, user groups, publications.

Gather data in relation to stated needs/objectives and in time to be useful; confine initial surveys (user requirements, site) to bare essentials, and to data that are readily available and immediately useful. Balance the penalty of insufficient information against the cost of obtaining it. Store data in a flexible way so that new information can be added readily.

Different techniques may be needed for obtaining different types of data: for summaries of the main methods see Appendix A.5.

Existing building(s): survey

Where applicable, survey/appraise existing building(s): premises presently occupied to be altered/extended or new premises to be converted.

— measure up and prepare survey drawings.

— investigate construction, materials, elements, finishes, services.

— prepare report on all defects including cause and recommended method of correction.

In premises presently occupied, how is client accommodated now? This is useful as basis for comparison even when new building is being planned.

Determine:

— how the building has been used through the period of occupation.

— the deficiencies and advantages in terms of the various users' needs.

— running costs, for example, maintenance, operation and changes.

Specific guidance on finding new premises is not given here. Specialist help may be required for the survey and report: to open up and examine foundations and structure; to trace services; to investigate rot, woodworm.

For outline of approach to evaluation of existing buildings see Appendix A.5.

Site

Where applicable, investigate site. If client owns specific site:

— visit and inspect.

— check if survey is available; if not, arrange for survey to be prepared.

If site is not fixed:

— investigate alternatives; determine appropriateness for proposed development.

— will owner sell? Is sale price reasonable: how does it compare with valuation by local authority? Are there any legal problems?

— make proposal based on analysis of potential sites.

The same basic technique is followed for both site selection and site survey/analysis. Appendix A.2 sets out the requirements in broad outline.

The survey and analysis is a very important part of the brief investigation and development. Data gathering can, however, be expensive and time-consuming and the survey must be well planned. It is generally advisable to employ the services of a qualified surveyor.

SECTION TWO
SPORTS AND RECREATION BUILDINGS

Introduction

2.1 General

Indoor facilities for sport have become an accepted part of everyday life in many parts of the industrialised world – particularly those countries which suffer from long periods of cold or wet climate, and long evenings of winter darkness. Some sports, such as badminton and squash, are played only indoors irrespective of the weather, and are becoming increasingly popular.

Most sports centres built in the past have been designed to provide facilities mainly for competition and training, and include both general purpose spaces such as sports halls as well as spaces specifically for one activity or range of activities, for example squash courts or ice-rinks. Indoor swimming-pools are usually included in these complexes because it has been found that their combination with the other sports facilities brings economic, management and user benefits. Not only can essential ancillary facilities such as car parking, reception, management accommodation, changing/toilet areas and refreshment spaces be shared, but there is also a saving in the amount of land required and a greater choice of activities under one roof.

In recent years people have gained more and more time for leisure as a result of a shorter working week, earlier retirement or forced unemployment. It has, therefore, become increasingly important to provide facilities in which it is possible for all – including the elderly and the disabled – to enjoy and participate in a variety of physical, recreational, social, and even educational activities. To meet these needs there is a growing tendency for sports complexes to cater for sport as a social activity for the whole family rather than a competitive activity for those in pursuit of sporting excellence. Such complexes provide facilities for people of all sporting standards linked to a wide range of cultural and recreational pursuits including music, dance, arts and crafts, drama, games and other hobbies and pastimes. There are usually areas for refreshment and social enjoyment to help promote a friendly and relaxed atmosphere. Facilities for competitive and spectator events tend to take a secondary role in this type of centre where multi-purpose function – for example, sports halls for dances, concerts and exhibitions – ensures maximum use of the spaces as well as bringing in extra revenue. The advantages of this must, however, be weighed against resulting compromise conditions for all concerned.

Sports can be played to various standards or combinations of standards – national, county, club or recreational. Only the largest facilities will satisfy all standards for all sports. The same standard need not be applied to all facilities in any one centre; one or two are often provided at a higher standard while many others may be provided at a lower standard. In a leisure-type centre a major difficulty is to strike a correct balance between those participating in sport seriously and those using the facilities for recreation.

Because of inflation, together with the shortage and expense of energy, it is becoming increasingly necessary to use resources in an economic way and this has influenced the manner in which sports and recreation activities are catered for. In Europe, the UK and the USA, more and more sports and recreation facilities are being jointly provided for, and used by educational establishments (usually schools) and the local community. Not only does this help to ensure fuller use of expensive plant and equipment, but the sharing of costs – for buildings, equipment, maintenance and staff – can also ensure the provision of better facilities and services for all. In the UK a study commissioned by the Sports Council has shown that joint-provision dry sports centres can be over 2.5 times more cost efficient than directly provided facilities, and those with swimming-pools about 1.5 times more cost efficient.

In the UK the number of sports and recreation centres grew from 50 in 1970 to 770 in 1983 and the Sports Council believes that in the next decade another 800 centres of all types will be required. It is anticipated that there will be a change in the pattern of provision during this period, with less emphasis being placed on the large, highly sophisticated centres presently being built, and more on smaller, flexible facilities – an attempt to strike a balance between the provision of large multi-function centres and small facilities which will be cheaper to build and which can possibly be managed by the local community. It also seems that more will be made of conversions of existing structures – particularly for the smaller community centres – and already there are a number of examples of this approach. Drill halls, railway stations, sawmills, church buildings and a former gaol have been rehabilitated and turned into sports and recreation centres.

The success of any centre will depend largely on:

— the involvement of potential users as well as relevant organisations at an early stage. It is, furthermore, important to keep them informed during the design and building process: awareness is an important influence on participation.

— the personality and organisational ability of the manager and his staff. A professional manager sees to the organisation and control of the premises and the programming and general running of the activities. It is important that this person be appointed at an early stage to assist with the formulation of the brief.

— a building which is distinctive in its special appeal. The major yardstick for measuring the success of the centre is its effectiveness in use: a leisure-type centre, for example, should provide a variety of facilities which people enjoy and return to time and time again.

— a building which is designed not only to permit efficient management but also to be economic to run and easy to maintain. A popular centre will be well used and therefore needs good quality construction, finishes and equipment which will be durable and keep down running costs.

— planned flexibility for future use so that the building may, over its lifetime, be added to, adapted or altered to meet changing user requirements and needs.

2.2 Types of client

There are various types of client for indoor sports and recreation facilities varying from full-time organisations or boards to part-time or spare-time sponsoring committees, associations or individual benefactors. The following broad groups of potential clients are found in most countries:

National and regional authorities
International, national and regional facilities for competition, training and coaching.

Governing bodies of specific sports
'Centres of excellence': specialised training and coaching facilities for the sport in question.

Local (or district) authorities
Sports and recreation facilities for use by all sections of the community.

Education authorities
Indoor games facilities in school buildings.

Universities and colleges
Examination/sports halls or sports centres; few are open to the general public throughout the day.

Government and institutional bodies
Sports and recreation facilities in hospitals, defence forces centres, and government departments for staff use.

Voluntary organisations

Usually the building is vested under trusteeship with the relevant national body, for example, the Young Men's Christian Association (YMCA). Site is often leased from the local authority.

Industry

Sports and recreation spaces within, or attached to, an office or factory; financed and run by the company.

Commercial

Specialised 'up-market' centres, for example, tennis halls and squash courts.

Private

For example, country clubs.

2.3   Types of building

National and regional centres

To train coaches and to provide facilities for top-class competition, training and coaching. Swimming-pools usually to Olympic standards and other elements suitable for international and national competition (regional centres for country or state-level competition) with adequate provision for spectators. A wide range of ancillary facilities, for example, lecture theatres, laboratories and residential accommodation, often form part of the complex.

Specialist sport centres

Usually built by governing bodies of a specific sport or, in some cases, as commercial ventures. A combination of sports may be included, for example, a racquet-sports centre – for tennis, squash and badminton – or a centre built specifically for the disabled. Some centres may also function, or be specially built, as spectator venues for sports such as snooker.

Sub-regional and district sports and leisure centres

For populations of 200,000–350,000 (sub-regional) and 25,000–90,000 (district). The catchment for district centres is a radius of about 6.5 km in heavily built-up areas, or approximately 20 minutes' travelling time for less densely populated areas. The centre usually consists of a multi-sports hall for use by all sections of the community together with ancillary activity halls or rooms. These facilities are frequently used for activities other than sports, for example, dances and exhibitions. It is often combined with a swimming-pool (a leisure pool generally requires a catchment area containing about 1,000,000 people) and other major indoor elements such as an ice-rink and bowls hall. A small theatre is sometimes included. Space standards and internal finishes are usually to full tournament requirements.

In some places this type of centre is being jointly provided by local education and town authorities. Local clubs may also participate. It may be built on a town centre site or further out and linked to a shopping centre or outdoor sports facilities. In country areas it may be linked to a network of paths used for walking, jogging, cycling or skiing. There may be co-operation between public and private sectors in the provision and/or management of such centres: they may be parts of large commercial developments, or certain elements may be operated by commercial organisations.

With the correct combination of facilities and efficient management it may be possible for income to equal overhead expenditure if capital repayments are excluded.

Local (or neighbourhood) recreational complex

For populations of 2,000–10,000 in limited catchment areas – all dwellings ideally within walking distance of the centre.

Facilities provided depend on population densities. Such complexes are usually more flexibly planned than district centres and offer facilities that reflect local needs and the character of the neighbourhood. There may be dual provision – with local education authority at primary school level and/or integrated with other neighbourhood facilities such as a library, health centre or shops. In this type of centre it is virtually impossible for income to cover running costs. Subsidies will therefore be needed.

Schools sports centres

For multi-purpose use for games (including gymnastics) but usually to practice standard only unless facilities are being provided jointly with local town authorities.

Other

Type and standard of facilities provided varies on function and purpose (see 2.2, 'Types of client').

2.4 Scope of guide

Although this *Guide* covers a wide range of sports and recreation buildings, emphasis is placed on community-type sports and leisure centres (at district or local level) intended for the relaxation of people of all sporting standards and providing a wide range of cultural and leisure activities. Much of the advice and information will, however, be appropriate for more specialised sports buildings.

Inception and initial brief

The object of this phase is to establish enough information about the clients' and users' overall requirements to allow the feasibility of the project to be assessed and to set the broad framework within which the design team is to work. The standard sequence of actions, starting with problem definition (1.6), should be followed initially. The steps described in 2.5 and 2.6 are supplementary and pertain specifically to indoor sports and recreation centres.

See Appendix A.1.a: 'Plan of Work', Stage A in *Architect's Job Book*.

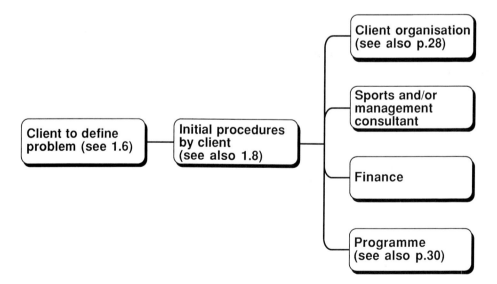

2.5 Initial procedures by client

Client organisation

If a local authority client intends to co-operate with a commercial operator who has not yet been identified, advice should be sought from experienced consultants. A list can be obtained from the Sports Council.

As the client is often a corporate body with a complex organisational and administrative network the client must define (and the architect verify):
— what the functions are (in terms of the proposed project) of the various departments, committees and officers who will inevitably be involved.
— what the responsibilities of all concerned are. This is particularly important in the case of two organisations collaborating in the joint planning of shared facilities. Ascertain, for example, who exactly is the client, who will be taking decisions, giving approvals and instructions.
— how the liaison between the client body, its own architects (where applicable) and outside consultants will function.

Sports and/or management consultant

It may not be practicable or possible to appoint a manager for the proposed centre at an early stage. In such cases it would be advisable to use management expertise on a consultancy basis. A list of consultants can be obtained from the Sports Council.

The client to decide whether a specialist building consultant is to be used. If so, ascertain position with regard to services provided, responsibilities, fees, etc. Investigate suitable consultants: check what sports and recreation centres they have worked on. Ensure that the selected person is appointed as early as possible.

Finance

See Appendix A.1.b: *Handbook of Sports and Recreational Building Design*[1], Vol. 1 p.147 or *Update: Indoor Sports and Recreation*[2] (23 March 1983, p.79). In the UK information on current policies and procedure can be obtained from the Sports Council or one of the regional councils for sport and recreation in England.

Consider method of raising funds:
— public organisation with power to make grants towards capital costs.
— joint venture such as co-operation between public and private sectors.
— commercial sponsorship.
— others.

Programme

Ascertain whether timespan for project will be determined or influenced by central government (or other) procedures controlling expenditure.

2.6 General data and objectives

While Section 2 provides specific information and guidance for the design of sports and recreation buildings, Section 1 offers guidance on the initial procedure basic to all design projects and should be referred to when considering general data and objectives.

Client's objectives and priorities

See 2.3; also Appendix A.1.b: *A Question of Balance*[3]. If a joint provision is being undertaken the philosophy, objectives and priorities of the organisations involved must be defined and agreed at the outset. See *Sharing Does Work*[4].

The client to define the type of centre required, the role it is to play in the life of the region, local community or of the parent body and, if a commercial venture, the market for which it is intended; also the relative importance of the main services to be provided, for example, competition, training, coaching, recreation, commercial, social and educational.

Determine other objectives both immediate and long-term and their priorities.

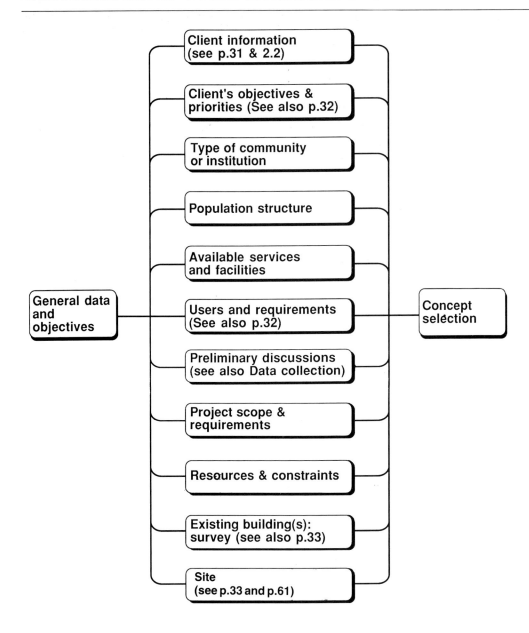

These may include some or all of the following:
—   to provide sports facilities for all levels of play and to make provision for
     spectators.
—   to accommodate the recreational requirements of various groups – the
     elderly, the unemployed, young families, etc.
—   to plan for maximum flexibility and multiple use of spaces with minimum
     effort.
—   to ensure that the design permits efficient management; also easy control
     and supervision of each activity.

— to provide attractive surroundings of high quality and durable finishes requiring only minimal maintenance.

Type of community

Information can be obtained from local authorities and other local organisations such as the Chamber of Commerce and regional council for sports and recreation.

Establish what type of community is to be served:
— rural and/or urban.
— catchment area – sub-regional, regional or small local community or Local Authority, etc.
— special characteristics.
— cultural and recreational patterns.
— local clubs and societies.
— plans and/or forecasts for future developments in the area.

Population structure

See census statistics and local planning department for population figures and details both present and projected. For general information on current trends in the UK see Appendix A.1.b: *A Digest of Sports Statistics*[5]; *Sport in the Community*[6].

Ascertain present and projected size of population in catchment' area. Also the characteristics of the population which have an influence on participation in sports and recreational activities:
— rich or poor area?
— habits and needs of inhabitants; also likely future changes.
— age, marital status, parenthood, physical disability, employment, income and car ownership.

Available services and facilities

Provision of recreation facilities for activities of local clubs and societies may be justified if unnecessary duplication is avoided.

Identify and investigate other factors that will influence the proposed facility so that overlap is minimised:
— available transport: public and private.
— existing and planned recreation facilities in or near the catchment area: location, extent and (for future developments) timing.
If a survey or study is to be carried out decide how this will be done and who will be responsible for the work.

Users and requirements

For a summary of briefing methods including questionnaires, surveys, etc., and for an outline of approach to evaluation of existing buildings, see Appendix A.5. Consult all relevant organisations including local sports and recreation clubs/societies, local residents' associations and neighbourhood/community councils, as well as individuals (for example community leaders) at the outset.

Consider the different types of users – various standards of sports players, recreational users, parents/housewives – and how the requirements of the various groups involved are to be determined:
— direct representation on the briefing and/or planning committee: delegates via local sports and recreation clubs/societies.
— and/or through questionnaire or local survey. If this method is to be used, ascertain who will undertake the work to formulate, distribute and analyse a questionnaire.
— and/or appraisal of existing sports and recreation centres with particular reference to users' comments.

Preliminary discussions

Once objectives have been defined, all interested parties identified and contacted, and basic data gathered, arrange meeting of all concerned with briefing process to:

— determine what further exploration should be undertaken.

— establish what specific services and facilities should be provided.

Note: what a community needs may be very different from what some members want or even demand. Not only must existing needs be determined but, in addition, an attempt must be made to forecast what is likely to change and be needed in future.

Project scope and requirements

The client/briefing committee must define the general scope of services, activities and facilities to be included; also, the emphasis that should be placed on each of them and the broad level of provision envisaged:

— which indoor sports and to what standards.

— swimming and diving pools.

— recreational and social facilities and other special requirements: multiple use of some spaces, crèche and play facilities for children of five to nine years.

— commercial facilities: shop, hairdresser, etc.

Consider whether all the necessary facilities and activities can be accommodated in one building without too many conflicts.

See 2.8, 2.11 and 2.12. Emphasis on facilities and activities will depend largely on the general function of the centre. Use information obtained from survey and consultations with assistance and advice from appropriate organisations: in UK, Sports Council or regional councils for sports and recreation. For a more detailed guide to the types of facilities and activities generally accommodated in different kinds of sports and recreation centres see Appendix A.1.b: Perrin[7].

Resources and constraints

Discuss and/or determine:

— availability of funds to meet capital, operational and maintenance costs.

— possible income to be derived from rentable space (shops, etc.) or hiring facilities to outside bodies or individuals (for dances, exhibitions, shows, etc.).

— limits of expenditure and the basis for computing costs.

— what, if any, outline approval/consents must be obtained and, if so, who will be responsible for doing this; also, what specific statutory requirements are applicable. Consult relevant bodies (national, regional or county sports authorities; licensing authorities, local authorities, etc.).

— what, if any, official standards are to be applied to the various sports facilities.

First costs – that is the cost of land, building, furnishing, etc. – become less significant (particularly in times of rapid inflation) when compared to future running costs – of operation, maintenance, repairs and replacements, etc. – during the life of the building (which may be expected to be 50 years or more). The main running cost is usually staff salaries and the other major item is energy. The latest information on trends, recent developments and standards can be obtained from the governing bodies of the various sports and from the national sports councils.

Existing building(s) survey

If project is conversion of (or addition to) an existing building, arrange for survey. Consider in particular:

— suitability of building for conversion to a sports centre in terms of the long spans needed, the ceiling heights, the need to comply with building regulations (for example, fire-escape stairs), flexibility and aesthetic appeal.

— the potential for future extension either vertically or horizontally.

— whether it will be reasonably easy and not too expensive to modernise/extend the services: power supply, heating and cooling, fire protection, lighting, etc.

Consent for altering use involves obtaining planning permission from the local planning authority. Application is usually made in two stages. The first, or outline, application to be made as early as possible. See Appendix A.1.b: *The Adaptive Re-use Handbook*[8] and *Saving Old Buildings*[9]; also *Sport for All in Converted Buildings*[10].

— the likelihood of unforeseen cost arising because of undetected defects/ problems.

In the case of an existing sports and recreation centre, consider:

— numbers of different types of users visiting the centre daily.
— how well each of the existing facilities is used.
— what facilities/activities need to be expanded or added.
— which existing facilities/activities could be reduced, combined with others or eliminated.

Determine:

— whether building is listed or in a scheduled area.
— whether it will be possible to obtain consent to change the use and/or alter the building.

2.7 Concept selection

The development of the brief is usually in progressive steps, in an increasing degree of detail. It is useful if this process is integrated simultaneously with the development of the building design so that there is interaction with the early design work. This will not only help to identify problems but will also lead to the testing of initial thoughts and the questioning of any preconceived ideas.

Consider the various *basic* strategic design concepts that are possible. Keep in mind in particular:

— stated objectives and overriding priorities.
— constraints (site, cost, etc.).
— circulation patterns: of users of wet and dry facilities, and spectators.

See Figs. 2.1a, b, c for a broad outline of various fundamental ways in which centres may be arranged.

There are no rules of thumb for initial rough estimating of floor areas required for sports spaces. For outline information see 2.25.

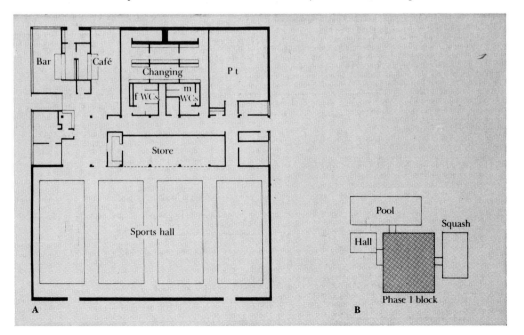

Fig. 2.1a *The SASH (Standardised Approach to Sports Halls) prototype is the result of a competition sponsored by the Sports Council. A: the basic unit. B: swimming-pool, ancillary hall and squash courts can be added without major disruption to users. (From* The Architects' Journal, *30 March 1983, p.51).*

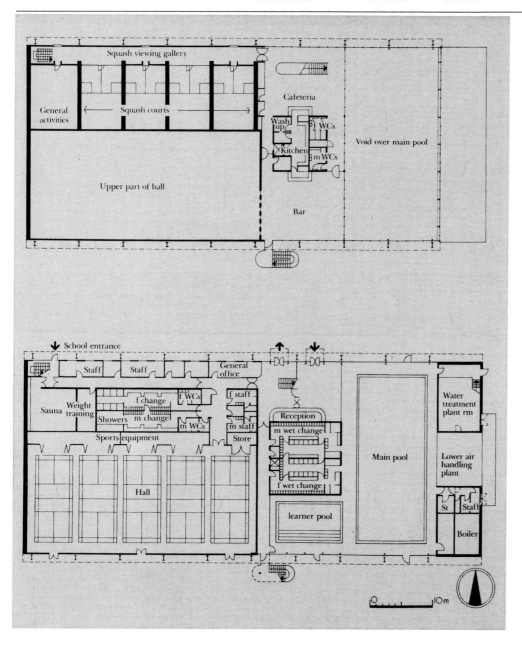

Fig. 2.1b *Example of large sports and recreation complex – Bletchley Leisure Centre – on three levels with major activity elements laid out around a central spine. (From* Handbook of Sports and Recreational Building Design, *Vol. 2, p.188.*

— easy control and supervision of all areas by minimum staff.
— massing: appropriate ceiling heights for the different spaces; single storey throughout or partly double storey.
— social areas which should, as far as is practicable, overlook the activity areas.
— flexibility required and allowance for growth.
— energy consumption/conservation.
— natural vs. artificial lighting and ventilation.

Fig. 2.1c   *Example of medium-sized complex –
Ringwood Recreation Centre – on two levels within simple
rectangle. Separate change-rooms are provided for dry and
wet sports. (From* The Architects' Journal, *20
October 1982, p.10).*

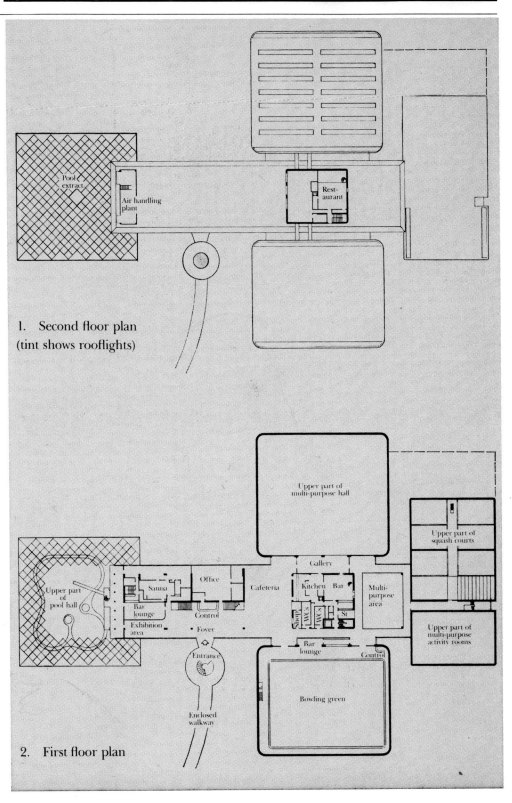

1.   Second floor plan
(tint shows rooflights)

2.   First floor plan

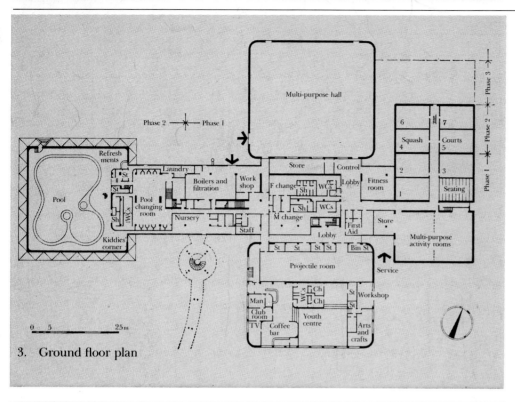

3.   Ground floor plan

2.8   Activities to be accommodated

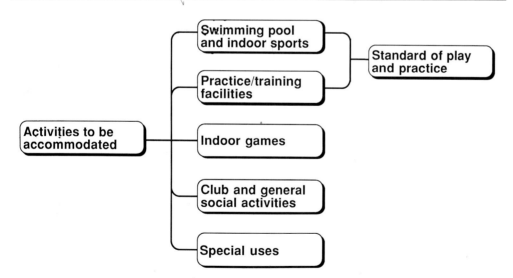

See 2.24.1 for checklist and basic information. See also A.1.b: *New Metric Handbook*[11], chapter 27. Care must be taken to ensure that sports, or groups of sports, to be included in the same hall/space are compatible. See also Fig. 2.2.

Swimming pool and indoor sports

Establish what sports are to be accommodated. Also type and number of pools, courts, pitches, enclosures required for each. In the case of special facilities (leisure pools, ice-rinks, etc.) consider:

— catchment area: because of high cost involved, accessibility to relatively large numbers of people.
— initial capital costs against likely level of income.
— additional maintenance costs for the sophisticated equipment required.

Assess sports types. For a community centre priority should be given to those which:

— have a low threshold of skill and from which enjoyment can be easily gained.
— require a low degree of organisation.
— have a relatively short activity period.
— can be undertaken over a wide age range.
— have social involvement: husband/wife, boy/girlfriend participate together.

Practice/training facilities

See 2.25.1.

Establish whether any special practice halls, training areas or warming-up strips are required: learner/training pool, gymnasium, etc. Determine whether such areas may be used for alternative functions: lectures, film shows, etc.

Standard of play and practice

See 2.25.1 and Appendix A.1.b: *Handbook of Sports and Recreational Building Design*[1], Vol. 2, p.46. Only the largest of facilities will satisfy all standards for all sports. The same standard need not be applied to all facilities.

Determine standard or level of play or practice for each sport. This will dictate floor area, standards of finishes and services, and the cost target:

— national and/or international.
— club and county (or state).
— educational.
— therapeutic or medicinal.
— recreational.

Indoor games

See 2.25.2.

Establish which games (if any) are to be provided for and the number and type of tables, boards, alleys required. Determine:

— which activities require separate spaces.
— which could be accommodated in one or more general-purpose rooms.
— which could be accommodated in sports areas.

Club and general social activities

See 2.25.2.

Decide what provision is to be made to accommodate general social activities. List anticipated activities (remembering that requirements will change over the years) and determine:

— which activities require separate spaces.
— which could be accommodated in one or more general-purpose rooms.

—   which could be accommodated in sports or games areas: spaces used for sports practice and training.

Special uses

Ascertain whether the recreational spaces will be used for any special community activities: discos, trade shows, exhibitions, jumble sales, fashion shows, etc. Consider that in spaces designed specifically for sport the lighting, acoustics and floors may not be suitable for certain other activities.

See 2.25.3. Multiple use of spaces will not work unless the required changes – of equipment, seating, etc. – can be made quickly and with minimal disturbance. See Appendix A.1.b: *Update*[2] (6 April 1983 p.79).

2.9   Management

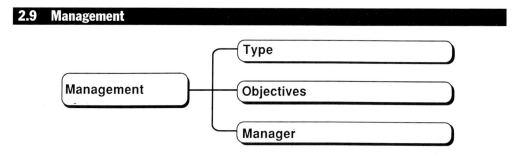

Various decisions regarding the management of the completed building must be taken at an early stage in the briefing process as they will determine some of the space requirements as well as the functioning of the centre; good facilities are not enough – good management is essential.

Type

Establish what type of management will be used for the centre: centralised management from the town hall – municipal sports' offices and club secretaries, with no 'on site' manager – or professional recreation manager possibly with assistants, or other system.

For more details of types of management, managers' duties, etc. see Appendix A.1.b: Perrin[12], chapters 1 and 12. Information can be obtained from the Sports Council, the Institute of Baths and Recreation Management and the Institute of Leisure and Amenity Management – see Appendix A.1.e.

Objectives

Establish primary aims and responsibilities of the management. These will be linked to the type of centre and local conditions. Determine:

—   extent of use by clubs and individuals.
—   whether participation by all age groups and people of all sporting standards will be encouraged.
—   opening hours.
—   whether there will be any automation to reduce staff numbers.
—   marketing methods such as membership schemes and promotions.
—   financial goals – any franchising to produce additional income.
—   educational programme: will courses of instruction be offered? Will centre be used by local schools?

Among the jobs of a full-time professional manager are arranging staff rotas, scheduling classes and clubs, ordering supplies, arranging publicity and sporting events (fashion shows, beauty contests, galas, etc.). The manager will usually try to be aware of local demands and may act as innovator by running courses in new activities so as to encourage and maximise use of the centre by the widest cross-section of the community.

Manager

If a professional manager is to be used he/she should, if possible, be appointed at this stage to give advice on the arrangement of accommodation and probable pattern of use; and to assist with the coordination of requirements of various groups of future users, and fund raising (if required).

2.10   Pattern of use

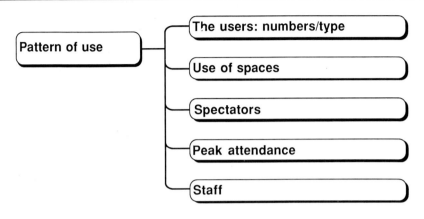

Determine the broad pattern of use envisaged and establish numbers and types of people involved. These factors will affect the amount of changing accommodation to be provided, and the size and arrangement of the ancillary facilities.

The users: numbers

In some cases the sport or activity itself will determine the number, in others it must be assessed by the client, or his advisers and the architect.

Establish how many people will be involved as participants and how many as instructors or attendants for each sport and activity.

The users: type

See Appendix A.1.b: *Handbook of Sports and Recreational Building Design*[1], Vol. 1, Vol. 2 p.16: also Walter[13], Goldsmith[14] and Harkness and Groom[15] for information on the needs of the disabled. See Chronically Sick and Disabled Persons Act (1970) for statutory requirements.

Estimate age and sex of future users and any special characteristics. Consider:
— special provision for younger age groups: size of playing areas and equipment; changing-facilities.
— special provision for mentally or physically handicapped: door widths, toilet and changing-facilities; certain safety measures; access for ambulances to special side doors.
— extent of use by clubs and individuals.
— exclusive use of some facilities, at certain times, by clubs or priority to individual bookings.

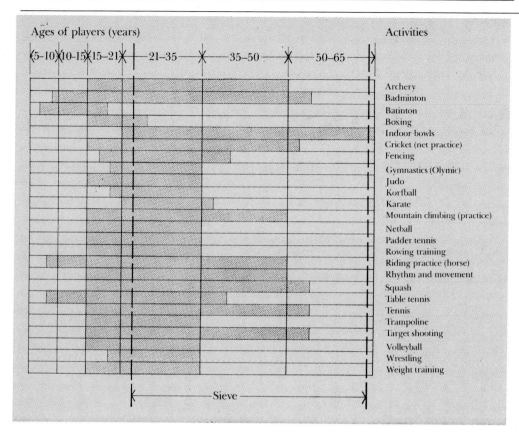

Ages of players (years)

|5–10|10–15|15–21| 21–35 | 35–50 | 50–65 |

Activities

Archery
Badminton
Batinton
Boxing
Indoor bowls
Cricket (net practice)
Fencing
Gymnastics (Olymic)
Judo
Korfball
Karate
Mountain climbing (practice)
Netball
Padder tennis
Rowing training
Riding practice (horse)
Rhythm and movement
Squash
Table tennis
Tennis
Trampoline
Target shooting
Volleyball
Wrestling
Weight training

Sieve

Fig. 2.2 *Sieve testing – one method of assessing and comparing the relative importance of indoor sports activities. Procedure:*

1 *List all activities to be considered.*
2 *Against this list set out a chart showing age ranges of players for each activity.*
3 *From population statistics for the area in question find the commonest age groups.*
4 *Plot the commonest age group on the age/activity chart. The completed chart gives the age groups for a wide range of activities. The sieve in this case shows the principal age group (24–63) for a seaside town.*

From this chart it is apparent that indoor bowls, squash, badminton, tennis, cricket practice and target shooting have most potential users in that particular town. In the absence of other factors these findings suggest that the requirements of these popular activities should be given priority over those of potentially less popular activities. It must be stressed that sieve tests give only a crude indication of demand. The most up-to-date population statistics may be several years old and any findings must be balanced against the probable future age structure of the area concerned. (From The Architects' *Journal, 10 March 1967).*

Use of spaces

Work out the pattern of participants' use of each major space. This is complicated when more than one group or organisation uses the same space. There may be:

— multi-use of the same space: one group following another playing the same or different game on same overall area.
— sub-division of space to accommodate simultaneously a number of different activities each requiring a smaller area.

Spectators

Ascertain what provision is to be made for spectators. Determine:

— frequency of use by spectators.
— type of seating (standing room may be considered): permanent or temporary. Check estimates given by client, sports bodies, etc. These often tend to be over-optimistic.

Activities may to some extent determine type and position of spectator accommodation; also the desirable maximum number. See 2.25.1. Popularity, standard of play, and duration of game will all affect spectator provision. Consider occasional use of other sport spaces for seating areas. See Appendix A.1.b: *Handbook of Sports and Recreational Building Design*[1], Vol. 1 p.90; Vol. 2 p.95.

Peak attendance

Determine periods of peak attendance and estimate numbers and types of users and spectators at these times.

Peak use: normally at weekends and weekday evenings when spectators are involved during special matches and tournaments. Peak time: usually mid- to late evening.

Staff

No general staffing levels can be laid down. Advice can be obtained from the Sports Council, the Institute of Baths and Recreation Management and the Institute of Leisure and Amenity Management. See Appendix A.1.e. Note: management and staffing costs represent a large proportion of the annual budget for running the centre. Building design must afford opportunity for economic staffing.

Determine management and staff structure as well as numbers and sexes, and whether full- or part-time, resident, club members:

— manager and administrators.
— typist/secretaries, receptionists, clerks.
— instructors and coaches.
— organisers and attendants.
— lecturers and teachers.
— doctors and nursing staff.
— waiters and other catering staff.
— plant engineers.
— cleaners, etc.

2.11   Administrative areas

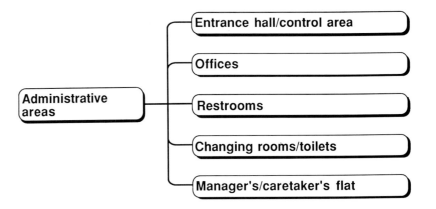

Entrance hall/control area

See Appendix A.1.b: *New Metric Handbook*[11] Chapter 6, and Perrin[12] pp.109, 110. See 2.25.4. Study entrance hall layouts and control systems used in existing sport centres.

Establish how public is to be managed, directed to facilities, served, informed and supervised. Consider:
— circulation routes through entrance hall/control area.
— method of booking, ticket-selling and control: reception window/counter between office and public area, automatic ticket machines at entrance.
— other facilities/activities to be provided for: windbreaks (vestibule lobby), hiring of equipment, queueing, waiting, display, advertising (leasing of wall space), public telephones, notice-boards, vending machines, publicity materials, storage.
— direct access to other areas: toilets, bar/refreshment area, rentable space (shops, sauna suite), etc.
— whether space is to be used for other activities on special occasions.
— separate entrances for: school children arriving by bus; disabled persons arriving by ambulance.

Offices

Establish administrative personnel numbers, duties and accommodation required:
—   personnel needing office space.
—   duties of each person in so far as they affect building planning: need own office/may share office? Adjacency to certain other staff members important/unimportant?
—   space requirements including storage.
—   special requirements: safe/strongroom, acoustic privacy from noise in sports hall, visual control, supervision of any public areas.

For sources of more information see 2.10: *Staff.* For details of planning and space requirements see Appendix A.1.b: *New Metric Handbook*[11] chapter 16, *Office Space*[16], and Duffy[17]. See 2.25.4.

Restrooms

Decide what form of social/rest area is required for staff: separate lounge-like space with facilities for tea-making, or will staff use public facilities? Determine scale of provision. This will depend on:
—   staff make-up: all full-time or mixture of full- and part-time.
—   maximum number of staff using area at any one time.

See 2.25.4.

Changing rooms/toilets

Determine requirements for staff changing/toilet accommodation:
—   no special provision; staff uses public facilities.
—   separate provision for males and females or shared facilities?
—   space requirements and number and type of lockers, showers, WCs, urinals and wash-basins.
—   special requirements: separate changing, locker and shower facilities for coaches.

See Appendix A.1.b: *New Metric Handbook*[11], chapter 38; also 2.25.4.

Manager's/caretaker's flat

Decide whether a flat for the manager/caretaker is to be integrated into the centre. If so, determine the space requirements, the relationship to other areas and the preferred position.

2.12   Social areas

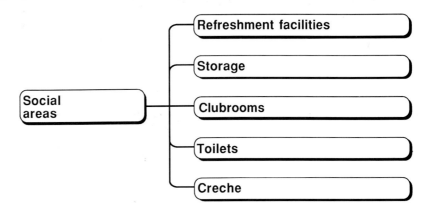

Refreshment facilities

Bars and restaurant can help not only to subsidise the sport and leisure elements but also to foster a more congenial atmosphere. On the Continent full restaurant service is common. In the UK catering is usually confined to snacks, confectionery and hot and cold drinks. For detailed guidance see Appendix A.1.b: *New Metric Handbook*[11], chapter 20; also Lawson[18], and Davis[19]. See 2.25.4. Information on local requirements should be obtained from the Health Department of the local authority. See Food Hygiene (General) Regulations (1970).

Consider need for and scale/type of refreshment facilities:
— restaurant; licensed bar; cafeteria; vending machines.
— form of service: waitress or counter?
— run internally or leased to a private enterprise?
— restaurant to operate independently (when centre is closed)?
— extent of patronage, for example by bathers in costume?
— special requirements: sited to overlook indoor activity areas; close to public toilets.

Establish ancillary facilities required:
— kitchen and/or other food preparation facilities; washing-up area; store(s) – kitchen, bar, vending machines; door to outside service area; refuse disposal.
— special requirements: bar store below bar; special security arrangements.

Advice can be obtained from local planning authority (also local magistrates or county court) and breweries. See Licensing Act (1964).

Bar facilities usually require licensing permission. Ascertain requirements and regulations for parking and toilets; fire and special security. If necessary, obtain outline planning consent and provisional licence.

Clubrooms

See 2.25.2.

Ascertain whether provision must be made for clubrooms. If so, determine:
— number; use to which they will be put: meetings, seminars, film shows, etc.
— dual-purpose: flexible spaces or used for other activities?

Toilets

For guidance on the standard of provision see BS CP 3 chapter VII; also Appendix A.1.b: *New Metric Handbook*[11], chapter 38. See 2.25.4. Consult the local authority.

Determine provision of toilets for spectators and visitors; also in support of refreshment/bar areas.
— numbers: male and female.
— special requirements: for licensing permission; for disabled.

Crèche

If facility for child-minding on casual basis is required, consider:

— how many children to provide for.
— special requirements: toilets and washing facilities, pram storage, storage for toys, etc.
— shared use: with committee or clubroom.
— possible provision for older children: five to nine years old.

Provision will encourage regular use of the centre by young mothers and parents of young children. Advice can be obtained from local authority social services department. See 2.25.4.

2.13 Ancillary areas

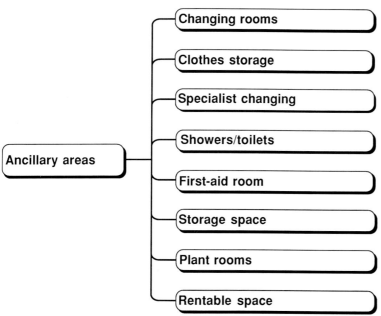

Changing-rooms

Decide on scale and system of provision. Consider:

— wet and dry sport changing areas combined/separated?
— numbers of different types of users at peak periods.
— cubicles: open-plan or combination of both?
— if cubicles, mixed changing or separate areas for males and females? Is wet and dry system to be adopted?

Consider:

— separate provision for outdoor facilities (if applicable) and for squash courts.
— flexibility to meet differing proportions (male/female) and needs (clubs, sports teams): for example, system of interchange rooms.
— special requirements: the disabled; family changing-cubicles; provision of hairdryers; hairdressing facilities.

Flexibility is advisable to meet varying needs; a mixed central area with cubicles is most flexible to cope with male/female use. For more detailed information see 2.25.4 also Appendix A.1.b: *Handbook of Sports and Recreational Building Design*[1], Vol. 1 p.87, Vol.2 p.91 and Dawes[20], chapter 11.

Cubicles and lockers provide the best all-round facilities. Communal clothes storage unit area equals total locker area, is cheaper to equip but needs extra staff and is more expensive to run. For more detailed information see 2.25.4; also Appendix A.1.b: *Handbook of Sports and Recreational Building Design*[1], Vol. 1 p.88 and Dawes[20], chapter 11.

Clothes storage

Decide on scale and system of provision. Consider:
— individual cubicles, lockers or hangers/baskets with central store.
— if central store, can it be combined for both sexes and differing groups of users?
— size of store(s) or number and size of lockers/cubicles.
— provision for storage of bulky items: sports bags and equipment.

Generally the more changing is grouped together, the better the supervision and flexibility.

Specialist changing

Consider provision of separate change areas for coaches/instructors of both sexes and for special use (visiting artistes, mannequins, etc.):
— number and type required.
— additional facilities: lockers, showers, toilets etc.

Communal showers are acceptable for males; individual stalls are preferable for females. For more detailed information see 2.25.4; also Appendix A.1.b: *Handbook of Sports and Recreational Building Design*[1], Vol. 1 p.89 and Dawes[20], chapter 11. For requirements of the disabled see Goldsmith[14] and Walter[13].

Showers/toilets

Ascertain requirements for toilets and showers for participants (bathers and dry sports) of each sex:
— facilities for dry sports and pool pre-cleanse area combined/separated?
— number and type (communal or individual stalls) of showers.
— number of WCs, urinals and wash-basins.
— special requirements: disabled.

Consult local health officer and/or St. John's Ambulance Brigade for requirements: planning and equipment. See 2.25.4.

First-aid room

Consider provision of room(s) equipped for the treatment of serious injuries sustained in both swimming-pool and dry sport facilities:
— equipment to be included – life-saving appliances, couch bed, wash-basin, medicine cabinet, etc.
— dual use of space for other approved activities – massage, physiotherapy.
— special requirements: direct access for ambulance.

Storage space is frequently under-estimated and should be carefully considered. Chemicals must be stored separately; specialist advice should be obtained on the safe storage of materials. See 2.25.4.

Storage space

Establish exact requirements for each activity:
— list equipment: critical dimensions; methods of storage.
— special needs: storage in one piece (or sections) of large elements such as trampolines, bleacher seating, platforms; also storage of chemicals.
— storage for ancillary elements: tables and chairs, netting, ropes, visual aids and cleaning equipment.

Discuss with specialist consultants, manufacturers at early stage. For more detailed information see Appendix A.1.b: *Handbook of Sports and Recreational Building Design*[1], Vol. 1 p.93, Dawes[20], chapters 13, 14 and 15 and Perkins[21], chapter 7; also 2.25.4.

Plant rooms

Determine need for and approximate space requirements of:
— gas meter; oil storage tank; coal bunker; LPG installation (usually outside the building).
— swimming-pool filtration, disinfection and heating.
— boilers and other space heating plant.
— ventilation/air treatment plant.

— electrical sub-station and emergency installation.
— water-storage tanks.
— workshop.
Consider location of spaces:
— basement.
— ground level.
— roof.

Rentable space

If rentable space has to be provided determine scale; also scope of architect's responsibilities. Consider:
— shops: for example, selling sports goods.
— hairdresser, beautician, launderette, etc.
— sauna and solarium if these are not 'in house' provisions.

2.14   General considerations

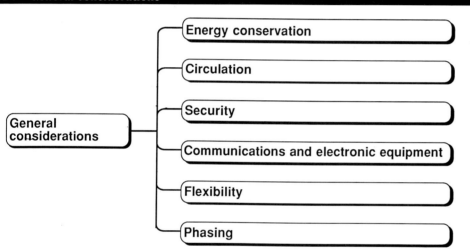

Energy conservation

Consider energy requirements and possible conservation:
— what fuel(s) will be used?
— solar energy; heat pump and/or heat reclaiming devices?
— could building be connected into a district heating system?
— insulation and control of infiltration.

See Appendix A.1.b: Dawes[16], chapter 14.

Circulation

Check on required pattern of movement through building for the following:
— the different types of users: give special consideration to needs of disabled persons and mothers with prams – passage widths, space for parking wheelchairs and prams, ramps and gradients, etc.
— the staff.

See Appendix A.1.b: Walter[13] and Goldsmith[14]; also *New Metric Handbook*[11], chapter 6.

— materials and equipment: goods entrance, passage widths for movement of equipment – for example, mobile seating units between activity areas.

Security/control

Discuss with licensing authority, local fire department and police. See Appendix A.1.b: *Thinking About Fire*[22] and *Security in Buildings*[23].

Ascertain broad requirements with regard to:
— number and position of exits and fire-escapes; also control points.
— fire-alarms; fire-fighting installation and/or equipment.
— burglar alarms.
— anti-vandal measures: use of closed-circuit television.

Television and radio

Discuss with television authority/company. The local authority should be approached regarding safety requirements. See Appendix A.1.b: *Handbook of Sports and Recreational Building Design*[1], Vol. 2 p.153.

Determine whether provision must be made for television and radio broadcasts. If so, consider:
— permanent commentator's box in main spaces.
— space required for scaffolding platforms and camera dollies.
— access for cables and equipment.
— special requirements: parking for TV vehicles; power and lighting.

Communications and electronic equipment

Discuss with telephone authority and relevant consultants/specialists (manufacturers/suppliers of electronic equipment). See *Telecomms Users' Handbook*[24] and *Communications*[25].

Ascertain what provision must be made for:
— signalling and public address systems.
— internal telephone system and GPO for both staff and public.
— clocks; electronic scoreboards and timing devices; control room(s).

Flexibility

Care must be taken that efforts to provide too much flexibility do not result in a building with no character and with a sterile atmosphere.

Determine extent to which flexibility must be planned for. Consider:
— space for undetermined use at outset; other solutions to possible long-term needs.
— multiple-use of certain spaces and effect on equipment (easy to dismantle) and storage (easy and accessible).

Phasing

If centre is to be built in stages, consider:
— priorities for each element.
— method of planning to permit building to remain in use continuously.

2.15 Site

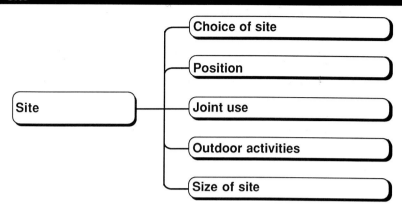

Choice of site

If site already chosen check that:
— client has ascertained that it is suitable.
— alternatives have been investigated.
— general survey and feasibility have been undertaken.
— outline planning approval has been obtained.
If site not yet selected, investigate possible alternatives.

See Appendix A.2 for information on analysing chosen site or evaluating possible sites. When considering cost of site keep the following in mind in addition to initial outlay:
— rates and taxes.
— effect of topography, soil conditions, etc. on building and landscaping costs.
— possible cost of providing certain services on site.

Position

Check/ensure that the site is:
— safely accessible – by foot, bicycle, car, public transport – from all parts of the catchment area.
— in a prominent position.
— well situated to serve schools.

It is important that children be able to reach the centre easily and safely.

Joint use

Try to relate centre to other facilities on same/adjacent site (schools, shops, etc.). If joint provision check that centre can be so sited that:
— community use does not conflict with other use (for example, school).
— it will be clearly and easily identified by public.

A combination of facilities on the same/adjacent site is desirable as it increases casual use of activity and refreshment facilities.

Outdoor activities

If there are existing or planned outdoor activities on the site in question, determine:
— envisaged relationship to proposed building.
— effect on provision of changing-rooms, toilets etc.

Size of site

Establish that site is large enough for:
— estimated accommodation.
— expansion, parking, outdoor activities and landscaping.

Feasibility

See Appendix A.1.a: 'Plan of Work', Stage B in *Architect's Job Book*.

This phase is concerned with a study and analysis of the data collected in the initial brief in order to reach a decision on the feasibility of the project. If feasibility has already been established before the architect is appointed, this stage should be used to check the client's assessment and conclusions, and to ensure that no factors have been omitted.

The depth of analysis and design sufficient to prove feasibility may vary considerably. The factors included here are only the basic essentials; where a more thorough study is required the more detailed information given under 'Outline proposals/scheme design' (pp.72-116) should be used.

2.16 Appointments

A design team containing people experienced in dealing with similar buildings can contribute to smooth running of the project. Approach relevant professional bodies for advice.

If not already done the architect and consultant should be formally appointed. Agree to:
—   clarify definitions of roles and responsibilities of all concerned.
—   clarify services to be provided by each member of the design team.
—   scale of charges.

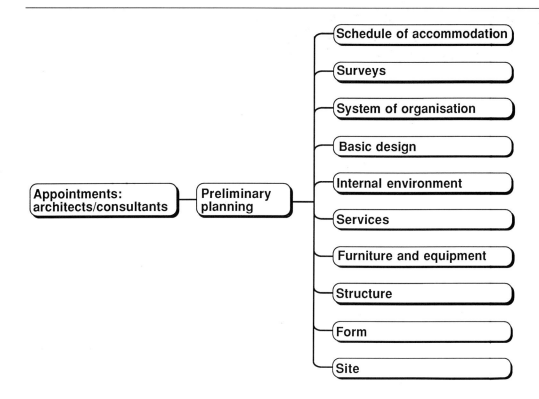

2.17   Preliminary planning

Schedule of accommodation

An outline schedule of accommodation should have been drawn up during the previous stage. Now:
—   check schedule; compare accommodation with known examples.
—   determine floor areas for each of the individual spaces.

For basic information on floor areas for sports and other activity spaces see 2.25.1-4.

Surveys

Identify sources of information:
—   survey current literature specifically relevant to project.
—   prepare list of references as a working document.
—   investigate/visit related projects.

For list of references see Appendix A.1; for outline of approach to evaluation of existing buildings see Appendix A.5. Useful sources include AJ Annual Review (including bibliography) and Guide to Information Sources (usually published during January); also Architectural Periodicals Index from RIBA Publications.

System of organisation

Confirm what system of organisation is to be used in the new building. Consider:
—   form of management and number of staff.
—   number and type of control points.
—   patterns of use and programme of activities in the various spaces.
—   basic space relationships: activity areas, social areas, service areas, etc. in relation to one another and to circulation areas/elements.

See Appendix A.5 for outline information on interaction matrices, etc.

Fig. 2.3 *Diagrammatic relationships between main elements in a large sports and recreation centre. (Basic diagram from* The Architects' Journal, *10 May 1967).*

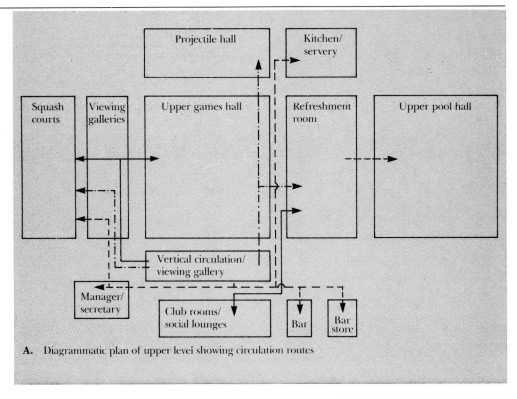

A. Diagrammatic plan of upper level showing circulation routes

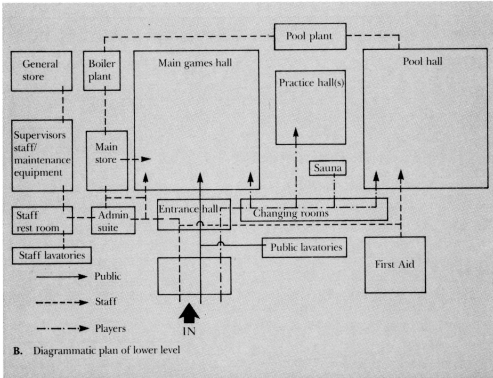

B. Diagrammatic plan of lower level

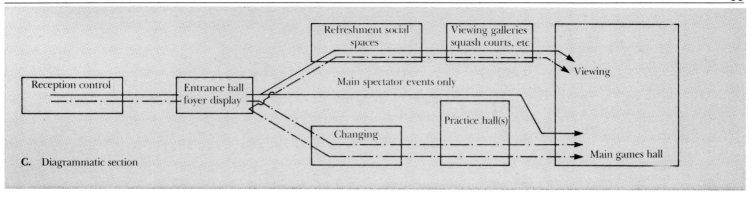

C. Diagrammatic section

Prepare:
— flow charts.
— interaction/relationship matrix.

Basic design

Work out approximate form of building. Prepare several alternatives. Consider the following:

— building regulations and other special legislation affecting siting, design and construction.
— zoning: relationship between main elements of complex; consider alternatives.
— visual relationships: main entrance; refreshment areas overlooking activities; spaces requiring privacy, etc.
— circulation and control: flow and separation of participants and non-participants; corridors; vertical circulation; easy control and supervision of all activities by staff, etc.
— external vehicular access: position of areas needing direct access – deliveries, ambulance; parking.
— orientation: in terms of heat gain and loss; view (from swimming-pool); prevailing winds (windows and entrances), etc.
— fenestration and/or rooflights and how their provision/omission will affect ventilation, lighting, heat gain and loss, construction and appearance.
— environmental control: position of spaces likely to become overheated, and noisy areas (squash courts).
— flexibility and phasing: position of areas to be added or extended in future.
— relationship with adjoining facilities.

There should be no premature bias towards one single solution. Alternative solutions should, at this stage, be kept geometric. For basic information on space and activity relationships see 2.25.1-4; see also Fig. 2.3.

Internal environment and pool

Determine broad requirements for:
— heating, cooling and ventilation.
— lighting.
— acoustic control.
— filtration, disinfection and heating of pool water.

Consult appropriate specialists, manufacturers and suppliers. Keep in mind that the cost of the services installations will be between 25 and 33 per cent of the capital costs; maintenance costs will be significant.

—   protection systems, etc.

Consider in particular:

—   the degree to which internal energy will be recycled, for example, waste heat recovery.

—   the flexibility/adaptability required in the degree to which comfort and lighting must be suitable for sports as well as other activities.

Investigate alternatives which will be most appropriate for:

—   each of the layouts selected.

—   the different types of spaces.

—   the structural systems under consideration.

Services

Discuss with local authorities, supply-boards, etc. The location of plant rooms and main distribution runs (vertical and horizontal) must be considered together with the structure at an early stage if services are to be satisfactorily integrated.

Ensure that adequate supply and disposal services will be available:

—   water supply and pool drainage.

—   electricity: will a transformer be required? If so, how much space will be needed?

—   waste disposal: estimate how much waste will accumulate weekly. How will it be stored and removed?

Consider:

—   communication systems: internal and external telephones, public address, etc.

—   protection systems (fire and security) and effect on design.

—   integration and distribution of services: position of distribution boards and plant rooms to keep runs to a minimum; compatability with structural systems.

—   flexibility: lighting for multi-purpose use of spaces.

Equipment

Equipment can influence planning, structure and cost can be 12 to 15 per cent of capital costs. Consult manufacturers of sports/gymnasium equipment.

Ascertain what fixed equipment must be included. Check:

—   dimensions and weights.

—   methods of fixing.

—   costs.

Structure

Keep in mind that single-storey has the economic advantage of allowing the use of lightweight structures for long spans. See Appendix A.1.b: *Update*[2] (6 April 1983 p.75).

Investigate structural possibilities for the alternative layouts. Consider:

—   whether the building will be single-storey throughout or double-storey in parts.

—   heights and large spans required in some spaces.

—   legislative constraints.

—   ground conditions.

—   fittings/equipment fixed to or suspended from roof structure.

—   problems of humidity and chemical environment (condensation and corrosion) in pool hall.

Form

Develop the massing of the various layouts (probable building shape) and relate to site and adjacent buildings. Consider:

— whether requirements of internal spaces (form/volume and relationships) have been taken into account.

— problems of scale created by large volumes and/or shape required: pool and sports halls, and squash courts.

— suitability for expansion.

— suitability for ventilation and lighting systems under consideration.

— town planning regulations.

— cost: economy of surface to volume ratio.

Discuss with local authority; landscaping (earth mounds or lowering of the building into the site) may be required to relieve the scale of the complex.

Site

Check that each of the layouts fits the site. Keep in mind:

— expansion.

— outdoor requirements.

— adequate access.

2.18   Cost planning

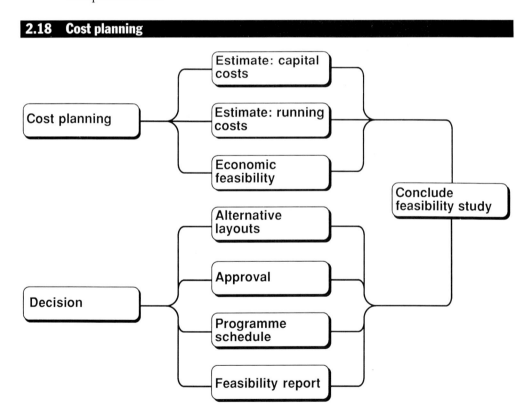

Estimate: capital costs

Obtain estimates of capital costs of alternative layouts from quantity surveyor: include all professional fees and expenses. Determine:

— apportionments.
— loan charges; length of repayment period.

Estimate: running costs

Staffing costs usually amount to more than 50 per cent of total running costs. Correct decisions and careful planning can assist in reducing supervision and cutting staff costs. Consult person appointed as manager.

Prepare outline of probable running costs. Consider:

— alternative solutions with regard to operational methods and likely effect on running costs: numbers of staff needed.
— maintenance of building, equipment and services.
— energy consumption: fuel for lighting, heating, etc.
— likely income.

Economic feasibility

It is important to determine feasibility in relation to life-cycle costs and not just capital costs. The latter become less significant when compared to running cost over the estimated life of the building. This is particularly true at times of rapid inflation. See Appendix A.1.b: *Update*[2] (6 April 1983 p.69).

Balance financial needs and resources; determine economic feasibility.

2.19   Conclude feasibility study

Alternative layouts

Discuss alternatives with all interested parties. No one layout will represent a solution; several may confirm criteria which final solution requires.

On the basis of foregoing studies and comparative analysis:

— select best alternative solution to building layout.
— prepare final proposal based on several alternatives.

Approval

Obtain approval of development in principle from local authority.

Programme schedule

Check sequence of operations with all members of design and client team. Discuss implications and adjust overall programme and resource allocations if necessary to balance time needed with time available.

Prepare revised programme schedule. Determine:

— earliest and latest dates for starts and completions of each stage for each aspect of work.
— resource implications affecting programme: finance, bank loans, accommodation for design office.

Feasibility report

Prepare report on feasibility of project, including proposals, in terms of:

— client's stated requirements.
— site limitations.
— complete financial implications, making clear relative allocation of costs to building fabric, services, furniture and equipment, landscaping, professional fees, etc.

—   structure, services, etc.

Note any modification that should be made to the brief.

Decision

Submit report for consideration to client. A decision must be taken:

—   to proceed, or
—   to modify requirements and reassess feasibility, or
—   to abandon the project.

Detailed brief

This stage is concerned with setting out a detailed brief covering all the major factors with which those involved in the project must be concerned. It represents amplification of and addition to the broad issues discussed in the primary brief. Its form is usually written and diagrammatic and emerges over periods of extended talks with the client, the design team and the users.

Further design work may start before the completion of a full brief and certain studies suggested under 'Outline proposals' may have to be made before the secondary brief can be finalised. This brief will, obviously, require review and, inevitably, amendment and revision as the work progresses.

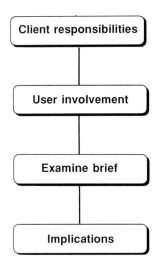

2.20   Client responsibilities

Ensure that the client provides, or helps to provide, data on detailed requirements. Discuss design implications, for example, in relation to operational and management policies.

2.21   User involvement

Ensure that the ideas developed up to this stage are made available to the local community (and other users) for comment and reaction. This can be done through:
— the local press.
— an exhibition or booklet.
— community meetings.
— sports and recreation clubs.

It serves no useful purpose to publicise proposals when it is too late for future users to make positive contributions. Participation by them in the production of the brief ensures commitment to the subsequent design and an understanding of the completed project.

2.22   Examine brief

Proceed to:
— check that all items listed under initial brief and feasibility have been considered.
— list any outstanding items about which decisions have yet to be reached or research initiated.
— examine basic changes in requirements for their effect on previous feasibility judgements (Note: costs).

The various specialists (including manufacturers or suppliers of specialised equipment) must be asked to consider the implications of the up-to-date brief as it affects their particular responsibilities.

2.23   Implications

Consider implications of the detailed brief with regard to:
— previous decision.
— contracting methods.
— the project programmes as a whole.
Revise the programme if necessary; advise the client and other relevant persons/bodies of any changes.

Outline proposals/ scheme design

This phase determines the general approach to layout, design and construction, which is developed to the point where one definite scheme (together with cost analysis) is produced and agreed upon by all the consultants and put forward as a recommended solution to the client. This stage may well have been reached by the end of the feasibility period, and may therefore be the confirmation of any already fairly detailed solution but incorporating any modification found necessary while preparing the feasibility study and detailed brief.

If the feasibility phase was bypassed, the factors outlined in that phase should be consulted for a broad appreciation of the size of the problem and as a quick check on the feasibility of the client's more detailed requirements now available.

2.24   Detailed information

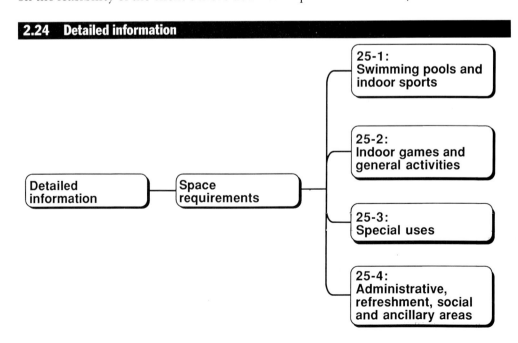

Studies undertaken in broad terms only at earlier stage must now be carried out in detail:

— site studies.
— study of similar projects.

2.25   Space requirements

Assess space and design requirements for individual elements:

— pools and indoor sports.
— indoor games, social activities and special uses.
— administrative areas.
— refreshment facilities.
— ancillary areas.

For each space list the following:

— nature of activities performed there: flow/circulation patterns; quiet or noisy, etc.
— relationships to other spaces/functions.
— type and number of playing spaces and users (participants and spectators) to be accommodated.
— special requirements: control or supervision.
— equipment and storage requirements.
— requirements for services, lighting, heating, acoustics, etc.
— provision for flexibility/adaptability and for expansion.

1 Swimming-pools and indoor sports

Types of pool
Competition/multi-use pool: swimming races are based on multiples of 100 m. Preferred lengths of pool are 25 m and 50 m; in the UK 33⅓ m is also used. Width is determined by number of lanes (each 2–2.5 m wide); competition pools are usually 6, 8 or 10 lanes wide plus 500 mm on each side of outside lanes.
Common sizes:

International	50 m × 21 m (25 m preferable)
National/regional	50 m × 13 m or 17 m
County/district	33⅓ m × 13 m or 17 m
Club/county	25 m × 13 m or 17 m

Free-form leisure pool: this type of pool is often designed as a fun or pleasure centre and may include wave-making machines, 'islands', recreational chutes (slides), as well as large surrounds with internal landscaping. In some cases provision is made for surfing. Size and shape will be influenced by equipment used and facilities provided. A 25 m pool with swimming lanes is sometimes incorporated within an informal shape: this must have parallel ends.
There seems to be no standard way of determining water area – the following can be used as a guide:

The basic requirements for each individual activity are given in 2.25.1-4. To save undue repetition certain detail information which may only be required at the following stage is included here. Note: standards for areas etc. must be seen as flexible guidelines to be adapted according to the type of centre and local needs. For detail requirements of ice-rinks and swimming-pools see Appendix A.1.b: *Handbook of Sports and Recreational Building Design*[1], Vol. 1; of indoor sports, *ibid.* Vols. 2 and 4.

In UK see also Appendix A.1.b: *Swimming Pools*[26].

Fig. 2.4   *Basic dimensions for competition pool. Note that lane lines are in centre of lane on floor of pool and must be in contrasting colour. (From booklet of Amateur Swimming Association – 'Swimming-Pools: requirements for competition').*

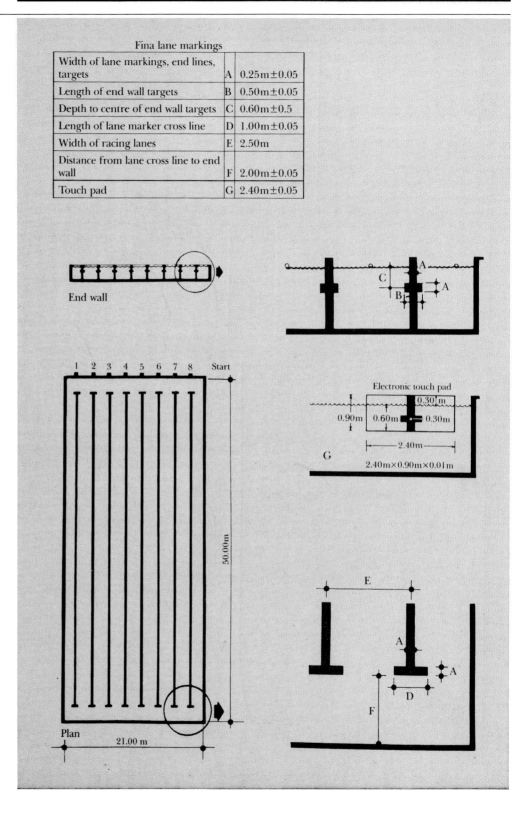

Fina lane markings

Width of lane markings, end lines, targets	A	0.25m±0.05
Length of end wall targets	B	0.50m±0.05
Depth to centre of end wall targets	C	0.60m±0.5
Length of lane marker cross line	D	1.00m±0.05
Width of racing lanes	E	2.50m
Distance from lane cross line to end wall	F	2.00m±0.05
Touch pad	G	2.40m±0.05

End wall

Electronic touch pad

0.90m   0.60m   0.30m   0.30m

2.40m

G   2.40m×0.90m×0.01m

Start
1 2 3 4 5 6 7 8

50.00m

Plan   21.00 m

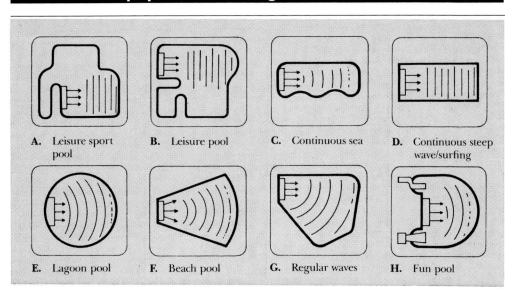

Fig. 2.5   *Typical shapes for leisure pools with wave machines. Any size or shape of pool can be accommodated and it is even possible to generate waves from an island situated, say, in the centre of the pool. The simplest unit requires a straight side for the generator plenum chamber (in the case of a pneumatic system), but the pool may have any desired shape. There must, however, always be a beach to absorb the waves and reduce reflection to a minimum. The height of the pool surround will depend upon the wave height, floor slope and pool shape. (From brochure of Armfield Engineering Ltd.).*

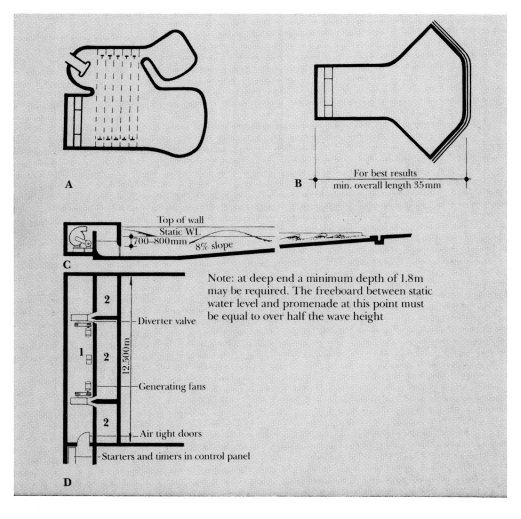

Note: at deep end a minimum depth of 1.8m may be required. The freeboard between static water level and promenade at this point must be equal to over half the wave height

Fig. 2.6   *Leisure pools and wave-making machinery. A: typical free-form pool with competition width and learner pool. B: typical formal fan-shaped pool with extended beach area. C and D: section and plan of pneumatic wave-generating installation. Two 60 hp fans are installed in the motor room (1) at the end of the pool, the compressed air from these is ducted through to the three sections of the forward chamber (2) via hydraulic shutters. Various types of waves may be generated. (From brochure of Biwater Filtration Ltd.).*

— 2–3 m^2 of water surface area per bather.
— 0.025 m^2 of water surface area per inhabitant in moderately populated areas (± 10,000 inhabitants) to 0.01 m^2 in densely populated areas (± 50,000 inhabitants).

Specialist pools: learner/training pool; diving pool; paddling pool. In Europe and the USA it is becoming common practice to provide multiple pool groupings: each pool is provided for a specific group of users. These are sometimes combined with the main pool using L, T or Z shapes but actual separation is safer and more manageable although cost is higher.

A learner pool can be virtually any size (for example 16⅔ m long) but if it is 20 m or 25 m long it is suitable for training use by swimmers. Width usually 8.5 m or 10.5 m. Normally kept shallow – about 750 mm – but if it is to be used for swimming training it must be a minimum of 900 mm. This size pool may be the only one included in very small local centres.

Instead of providing a diving pool, a 1 m springboard is sometimes installed in the main pool. Other boards should, for reasons of safety, have a separate pool. The Amateur Swimming Association (UK) recommends the following sizes:

— for 1 m and 3 m springboards   10.5 m × 10.0 m × 3.5 m deep
— up to 5 m   12.0 m × 12.5 m × 3.8 m deep
— up to 10 m   12.5 m × 15.0 m × 4.5 m deep

A paddling pool requires a water surface area up to 40 m^2 and a depth of 400–500 mm.

See Appendix A.1.b: *Swimming Pools*[26].

Fig. 2.7 *Diagrams illustrating movable floors and division walls in swimming-pools. A: movable floor with trailing ramp in multi-purpose pool – floor can be raised to any level by the four hydraulically operated pistons and can be given a slope. Provision is made (as shown) for cleaning below the movable floor. B and C: examples of two types of movable division wall. D: leisure-type pool with wave machine situated below pool floor in addition to movable floor and division wall. (Diagrams from A. F. W.-Bäder brochure from UK agent Buckingham Swimming-Pools).*

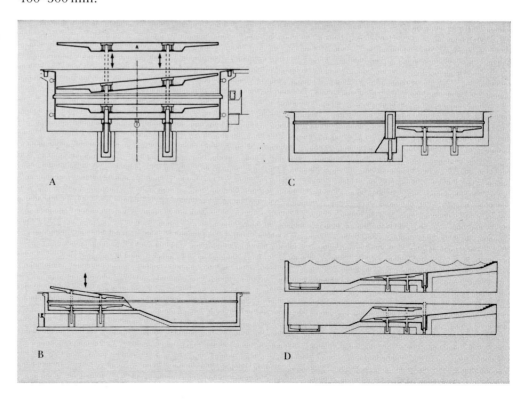

LAYOUT/DESIGN CONSIDERATIONS

For international/national competition, 1.8 m minimum depth throughout. Regional or local, usually sloping from 0.9 m–1.8 or 2 m. Problem: to determine extent of standing depth (1.2–1.5 m). A variable depth pool may be justified in certain cases. An hydraulically operated moving floor adjusts water depth to suit function (learners, recreational users, competition swimming, water polo, etc.); usually only part (about one-third) of floor. In leisure pools, depths will range from 1.5 m and over to zero up a gentle slope ('beaching' needed for wave machines).

For reasons of safety the hall should be entered at the shallow end of the pool.

Movable booms and bulkheads can be used to temporarily alter length or to partition pool into separate areas. (See Fig. 2.7.)

Elements such as springboards, slides, islands and wave-making machines require additional pool supervision.

A 1 m springboard in main pool increases depth (3 m minimum) and area of deeper water, as well the minimum width of surround at the board. More water area per bather must be allowed as use of board requires 45 m^2 (9 m × 5 m) of pool.

Learner pool should ideally be separated from but close to main pool. Provide broad steps along one side (or part of side) – as these are useful for introducing children to water. Minimum surround 2 m but provide enough space for casual seating for parents to watch children. Check whether temporary visual screening will be required at times.

Ideally diving pool should be 5–6 m from main pool and well away from shallow end. Boards should face a blank wall and not towards any activity where movement can cause distraction. Light must be controlled to eliminate glare. Agitators or sprays may be required to give ripple surface to water. Check on ceiling height required. Underwater windows may be required for coaching. Diving pools are expensive and often provided only in larger centres. Cost can be offset by using pool for sub-aqua, life-saving and synchronized swimming.

Pool(s) can be sunken or above ground, either partially or completely. Site condition (high water table, sloping ground or expansive clays) will help determine approach.

Site conditions can influence decision on construction of pool tank and specialist advice should be obtained. In situ reinforced concrete and reinforced gunite are widely used. Tanks can also be of precast concrete units, glass reinforced plastic (GRP), steel and aluminium.

As energy conservation is important pool tanks should be adequately insulated. Rigid polystyrene foams, expanded cellular glass and other materials can be used.

Various internal finishes are suitable: rendering and paint, Marbelite plaster, flexible heavy-duty plastic vinyl liners, rigid GRP membranes and traditional glazed ceramic tile or ceramic and glass mosaic.

Provision must be made for water overflow (scum channels or top-deck perimeter channels). Various systems are available: consult specialist.

Fixing bolts/holes for racing lane lines, starting-blocks, water polo goalposts, backstroke turn indicator, handrails, guard-rails etc. must be provided. Check with manufacturers for detail information.

Steps are normally recessed into the sides of the pool; they can be part of the structure or separate. If not recessed, they must be removable for competition. Asymmetric handrails are recommended.

Wave-making machines will have an effect on size, shape and pool-edge details: a minimum depth may be required at machine chamber. Check with manufacturer. Chamber requires thick walls for sound insulation.

Noise is a problem; reverberation can be reduced through use of planting, moisture-resistant acoustic ceilings, perforated bricks or tiles and by cushioned rubber tiles on surrounds.

Completely enclosed space can be claustrophobic but large glass areas can result in unpleasant specular glare, unwanted heat gain or loss, and problems with cleaning and breakages. Glare can be reduced in various ways including facing windows north (in northern hemisphere), tinted glass (not green), external screening or planting close to glazed areas, and underwater lighting. Safety glass must be used in low-level windows.

Condensation is a serious problem which must be overcome in indoor pools. Relative humidity maintained below 70 per cent, good ventilation, and proper insulation of walls, ceilings and windows (double glazing) offer the best means of control. Humidity and chlorine vapour adversely affect material and cause corrosion. Materials should be impervious; stainless steel, chromed brass etc. should be used for metal fittings.

Base of walls should be of robust, impervious, non-reflective material that can be easily cleaned e.g. perforated ceramic tiles. A light colour helps to provide pleasant, cheerful atmosphere.

Care must be taken in design and detailing of roof: in the past, corrosion has caused a number of roofs over indoor pools to collapse. If climate and cost allow it, various forms of innovative roof may be considered, for example slide or roll-away, or other forms of removable roof allowing virtually open-air swimming in good weather.

Lighting will vary with standard of pool: 300 lux at water level for training, recreational, club and county pools; 500 lux for national competition and diving. Underwater lighting may be required in leisure pools and a pacemaker system of flashing lights in the floor of specialised training pools (see Appendix A.1.b: *CIBS Lighting Guide*[27]).

Water temperature requirements for special pools may vary: for swimming 24°C minimum; for diving 26°C minimum; for learner pools 28–30°C. Air temperature in pool hall about 27–28°C. Consider use of ozone for water treatment to allow recycling of warm air.

For energy conservation consider:
— variable flow ventilation system.
— pool cover.
— heat recovery from extract air.
— recirculated air dehumidified by heat pump.

Power outlets/connections will be required for pool vacuum cleaner, electric clock, and electronic time-judging apparatus (touch panels, digital display boards, computer print-out, etc.), and possibly for TV. Check on other special requirements: underwater speakers, facilities for video filming, etc. Specialist advice should be obtained.

SPECIALIST POOL ACTIVITIES

Water polo: play area for national/international games $30\,m \times 20\,m$ with $1.8\,m$ minimum depth. For championship game 25–$30\,m \times 12$–$15\,m$ and $1.2\,m$ deep. For local club games $20\,m \times 8\,m$ and $1\,m$ deep is acceptable. Main pool or diving pool (if large enough) can be used. Goal-posts (which are $3\,m$ wide) must be light and portable; provision must be made for easily accessible storage.

Sub-aqua (scuba) diving: main pool or diving pool can be used. $1.5\,m$ depth is desirable ($1.35\,m$ minimum) and greater depths are sometimes required. If specialist tank is built, depth should, ideally, vary from 1.5 to $5.5\,m$. Bottom should be stepped rather than steeply sloped. For group instruction a minimum area of $5\,m \times 3.6\,m$ is required on a gradually sloping pool floor. If provision is made for a sub-aqua diving club and compressor room, workroom and equipment store will be required (area 25–$45\,m^2$).

Synchronized swimming: main pool can be used; diving pool is particularly suitable. Ideal minimum size $12\,m \times 12\,m \times 3\,m$ deep, but $250\,m^2$ pool area is preferred. Underwater lighting must be provided and should be connected to dimmer control. Underwater window is useful for coaching.

Canoe training: pool dimensions are not critical and the main pool or learner/training pool can be used. Depth should allow instructor to stand beside canoes. Provision may have to be made for storage and maintenance of canoes.

Life-saving: ideally some part of pool should have water depth of $2\,m$. Provision must be made for storage of life-saving equipment.

Pool surround area and sun-tanning area: the minimum widths of pool surrounds are $2\,m$, shallow end $3\,m$, at $1\,m$ springboard $4\,m$, and where pool is used for competition swimming up to $5\,m$ at start and finish end to allow for officials, etc. The total amount of deck space provided should at least equal the water surface area and a proportion of surround to water of up to 3:1 is ideal, particularly for leisure-type pools.

Storage: see 2.25.4.

Additional space may be required for one or more of the following:
— parking area for wheelchairs at shallow end.
— permanent spectator seating (where pools are to be used for galas).
— dry training area (trampoline and dry diving unit).
— recessed area at finish end for officials and equipment; also, possibly, adjacent rest-room for competitors.
— soundproof and air-conditioned room with unobstructed view of finish end if permanent computer equipment is to be installed.
— refreshment facilities accessible to bathers and spectators (leisure-type pool).

Consider opening up the pool hall to the outside (sliding roof panels or sliding walls) and/or providing direct links (electrically operated sliding windows) to outdoor pool where applicable.

Consider provision of sunbathing terrace or balcony off the pool hall. This should be properly sheltered and screened, and may be paved or of grass. A footbath may be required at door between hall and this area. Such a space should be closely linked to a paddling-pool and the refreshment area. Artificial sun-tanning areas (leisure pools) can be provided in sun-rooms or alcoves (see also 2.25.2, 'Solarium'). Consider provision of spectator seating: in relation to competitive swimming/diving area; space requirements, etc.

Consider position(s) of staff supervising pool area – an office with window through which entire pool area can be viewed may be required.

Main hall/dry sports

The range of sports provided for, and the level of play will determine the size of the hall. Standards vary from country to country. In the UK the Sports Council recommends the following basic sizes:

Flooring of surrounds must be textured non-slip and easy to clean and should be laid to 1:24 minimum fall. Floor material should look attractive either dry or wet.

Washdown hose points must be provided.

Seating can be fixed raking seating or bleacher seating for spectators. Bleachers can be wall-mounted retractable units or portable. Alternative is loose chairs – stackable or folding. Casual seating is usually required; warmed benches around pool hall are popular and useful for both the elderly and the disabled.

Drinking fountain(s) – preferably recessed into wall – should be provided.

Consider position of control unit for lighting, wave-machine, public address system; also life-saving equipment that may be required at the poolside.

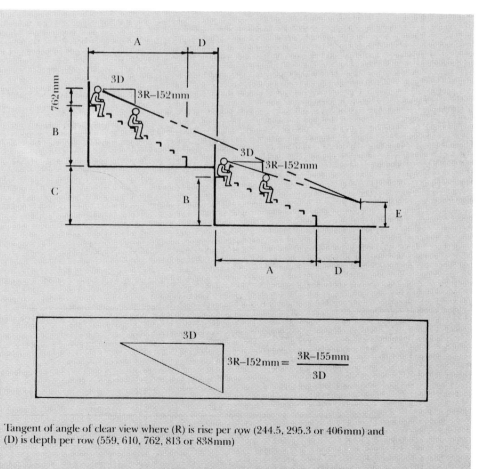

Fig. 2.8   *Basic sightline information. For best view, vertical dimension E, from court line to intersection of sightline, should be as small as possible.*

A: extended depth of seating.
B: overall seat height.
C: balcony height (should exceed B by approx one rise).
D: 1.2–1.5 m recommended (according to local code requirements).
E: vertical dimension from court line to intersection of sightline.

Angle of clear view (lower limit of sightline) is projected at eye level 150 mm over the head of the spectator seated three rows below. (From brochure of Hussey Seating Systems Ltd.).

$$3R-152\,mm = \frac{3R-155\,mm}{3D}$$

Tangent of angle of clear view where (R) is rise per row (244.5, 295.3 or 406mm) and (D) is depth per row (559, 610, 762, 813 or 838mm)

Fig. 2.9   *Proprietary seating systems. A. demountable seating in units 5.5 m wide and 4 or 8 rows in height; aisles can be fitted between unit sections. B: telescopic bench system with each unit fixed to the floor or wall. Unit widths range from 3 to 6 m and the number of rows from 3 to 20 m. C: telescopic seating. (From brochure of Audience Systems Ltd.).*

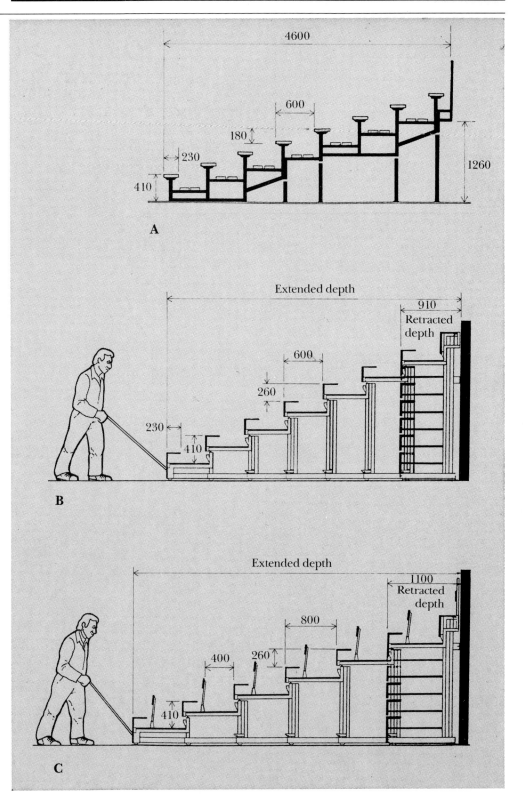

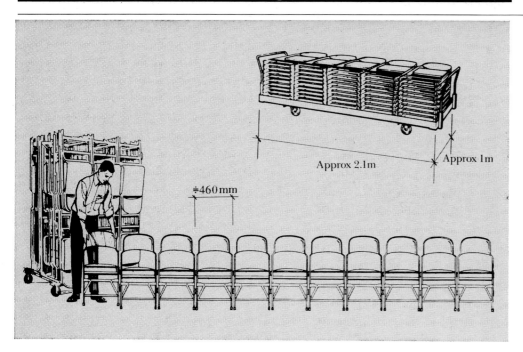

Fig. 2.10 *Flexible seating and storage system consisting of portable folding chairs (which can b[e] by brackets) and storage trolleys – two types are illustrated. See also Figs 3.87 and 3.88 on p.183. (Diagrams from Sandler Seating catalogue).*

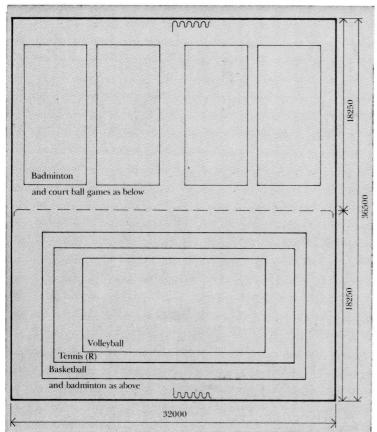

Fig. 2.11 *Size recommended by the Sports Council (UK) for a large sports hall. (From* The Architects' Journal, *14 June 1978, p.1176).*

Fig. 2.12 *Examples of the Internorm range of standard sports halls and pools adapted by the IAB (International Aquatic Board for Sports and Recreational Facilities) based in West Germany. Internorm complexes have been built throughout Europe and the USA. top:type B hall. bottom: size five pool for up to 50,000 inhabitants.*

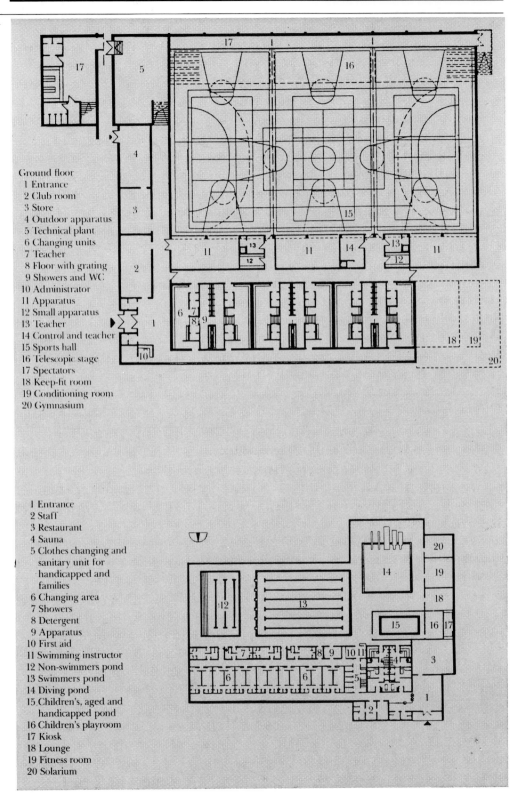

Ground floor
 1 Entrance
 2 Club room
 3 Store
 4 Outdoor apparatus
 5 Technical plant
 6 Changing units
 7 Teacher
 8 Floor with grating
 9 Showers and WC
10 Administrator
11 Apparatus
12 Small apparatus
13 Teacher
14 Control and teacher
15 Sports hall
16 Telescopic stage
17 Spectators
18 Keep-fit room
19 Conditioning room
20 Gymnasium

 1 Entrance
 2 Staff
 3 Restaurant
 4 Sauna
 5 Clothes changing and
   sanitary unit for
   handicapped and
   families
 6 Changing area
 7 Showers
 8 Detergent
 9 Apparatus
10 First aid
11 Swimming instructor
12 Non-swimmers pond
13 Swimmers pond
14 Diving pond
15 Children's, aged and
   handicapped pond
16 Children's playroom
17 Kiosk
18 Lounge
19 Fitness room
20 Solarium

Small local (community halls)
  17.0-20.0 m × 15.6 m × 6.7 m high (265–321 m²)
Small (for populations up to 25,000)
  22.5 m × 16.5 m × 6.7–7.6 m high (371 m²)
  26 m × 16.5 m × 6.7–7.6 m high (429 m²)
  29.5 m × 16.5 m × 6.7–7.6 m high (487 m²)
  32 m × 17 m × 6.7–7.6 m high (554 m²)
Medium (for populations up to 40,000)
  32 m × 23 m × 6.7–9.1 m high (736 m²)
  29 m × 26 m × 7.6–9.1 m high (754 m²)
  32 m × 26 m × 7.6–9.1 m high (832 m²)
Large (for populations up to 90,000)
  36.5 m × 32 m × 9.1 m high (1168 m²)
In West Germany the standard for small halls is 27 m × 15 m and large dividable halls are 45 m × 21 m or 27 m × 7 m high.

See also Appendix A.1.b: *Handbook of Sports and Recreational Building Design*[1], Vol. 2 p.46.

Ancillary/practice hall

This is often provided as back-up facility in support of main hall; specially for activities requiring small floor areas and relatively low ceiling heights, also for practice and recreational play. Combat sports (judo, karate, fencing) and table tennis as well as keep-fit, movement and dance, may use this space.

A hall 15 m × 12–15 m × 3.5–4.5 m high will be suitable for all these activities. A larger space, 21–24 m × 12–15 m, could be subdivided by a curtain or sliding/folding door to provide more flexibility. This hall may be used for some recreational activities such as dances, receptions, lectures and film shows. Storage could be combined with that of the main hall but certain specialist activities (movement and dance) may require separate storage space.

Many of the detailed requirements for this hall are the same as for the main hall. Full-length (2 m high) mirrors should be provided for fencers and for participants in movement and dance.

Blackboards and screens for projection are normally required. Ideally, these items should be designed to be concealed after use, for example by means of a sliding screen.

It must be possible to enter this hall without passing through the main hall.

Windows are not essential but desirable.

Decide on sports to be accommodated. Consider compatible activities and their space requirements including safety zones and spectator seating. Determine which sports will need to be played concurrently. Hall needs to be extremely adaptable and shape must permit maximum flexibility; wider halls tend to be more flexible in use. Tennis requires largest area: 32 m × 17 m minimum for one court; 2 courts for

The main factors influencing cost are shape, size and standard of finishes and equipment. Large halls tend to be more expensive because of greater height and spans; also shapes are often more complex and standards higher.
Structure must be given special consideration (fire requirements, wind-loading, and integration

of services: lighting, heating, and ventilation). Walls and roof must be sufficiently strong to support fixed or movable equipment and possibly large, heavy curtains used to subdivide the space. Wall surfaces must be flush and without projections or sharp corners. Walls must be capable of withstanding impact from users and of supporting the required equipment. Finishes should be matt, easily cleaned and non-abrasive for a height of 3 m above the floor. Walls may need to be visually and acoustically acceptable for leisure use functions. Above 3 m from floor level sound absorptive material capable of withstanding ball impact (e.g. woodwool slabs) may be used.

Access must be provided to reach high windows (for cleaning) and light fittings.

A variety of synthetic and natural flooring materials are available. Consider:

— the requirements and nature of the activities.
— joints must not affect playing performance.
— surface must give true and predictable bounce.
— must be non-slip – some sports (tennis) require a certain amount of 'slide'.
— light in colour but with matt surface to avoid glare.
— wear-resistant and easily maintained.
— ability to withstand heavy load such as bleacher seating.

Semi-sprung hardwood, PVC carpet stuck to chipboard or plywood underlay, foam-backed PVC carpet, and rubbers or plastics in sheet form or laid in situ are all commonly used.

Consider markings for various sports and permanent sockets for fixing equipment.

Ceilings should be sound-absorbent, capable of withstanding impact from balls, and light in colour. Consider the possible advantages of a flush ceiling. Although rooflighting is commonly used, consider the disadvantages: weatherproofing, sun-penetration, control of glare, heat loss and gain, cleaning, maintenance, etc.

Determine heating and ventilation requirements which will vary according to the activity and the season – winter temperature of between 13–22°C will be suitable for most activities. Air changes, 3–4 per hour – rate may need to be increased in summer if no provision is made for cooling. Warm air or radiant heating – or a combination of both – may be used. Care must be taken with the positioning of ventilation openings (windows, louvres, fans and/or inlets and outlets for a mechanical system) to avoid draughts on participants and spectators.

Lighting is extremely important. Decide whether daylight will be used or artificial light only; this can have significant influence on the form of the building. Lighting must be glare-free and even (average intensity at head level 350–400 lux). Some sports have very specific requirements (table tennis) and provision must be made for these. See Appendix A.1.b: *CIBS Lighting Guide*[27]. Consider flexibility of lighting to suit various activities.

practice play can be accommodated in a 36.5 m × 32 m hall with tournament play taking place in the centre of the hall. Where demand does not justify inclusion of tennis, approach can be more flexible.

Consider position of players' entrance from changing-rooms and their circulation routes to the various sports positions.

Consider entrance(s) for spectators, control point(s), emergency exits, etc. Adequate storage for the full range of equipment required by activities must be provided. Space should be shallow (not more than 5 m deep) and readily accessible, preferably along one of the longer sides. Area required will be between 50 m² (small hall) – 115 m² (large hall). Mobile seating will require additional storage space.

All doors and cupboards should be set flush with walls.

The hall may also be used for a wide variety of leisure activities: concerts, exhibitions, banquets and dancing (see also 2.25.2).

The hall may need to be subdivided at times by curtains or manually or electrically operated sliding/folding doors.

Sports types
Various sports can be accommodated in the main or ancillary hall.

Aikido: requires an area at least 9 m square with surrounding safety area of 1–1.5 m (2.5 m on one side to allow for officials). Suitable for ancillary hall. Storage required for mats on trolleys, officials' tables and scoreboards.

No special requirements.

Badminton: court size for all standards of play 13.4 m × 6.1 m. Provided the court has a minimum of 1.2–1.5 m of extra space around it, this sport may be played any-where in a common sports place. If possible, floor to ceiling height should not be lower than 7.6 m. Four courts can be accommodated in a hall 32 m × 17 m. Spectator seating can be all around court. There should not be any windows on walls at ends of court. Storage required for nets and supporting posts (±0.25 m² × 1.5 m long for each post). Two trolleys occupying 3 m × 3 m carry all the apparatus for four courts.

Important considerations: adequate height and lighting. Natural lighting should be from above (clerestory) and artificial lighting at least 5 m above floor and 600 mm outside the court as players are constantly looking upwards during play. See Appendix A.1.b: *Handbook of Sports and Recreational Building Design*[1], Vol. 4 p.7. End walls should have matt surface of medium to dark colour. A draught-free atmosphere is essential.

Basketball: court size 26 m × 14 m. The width may vary by 1 m and the length by 2 m but the proportions must be kept. Ideally, the court should have 1.5 m of extra space at each side and 3 m at each end. The floor to ceiling height should be at least 7 m (for recreational play 6.7 m is acceptable). Best view for spectators is from the sides; must be a minimum of 2 m from court. Storage space is required for two nets, their backboards and stands. For stackable type allow 6 m² × 915 mm each; for the fixed full-size type allow approximately 4.5 m × 2.5 m × 4 m high each.

Natural lighting from above. Artificial light sources should not be suspended below the ceiling.

Boxing: minimum dimension for amateurs is 3.66 m square. For competitions from 5–6.1 m (maximum) square. To allow for some spectator accommodation an area of at least 130 m² is required.
Can be in ancillary hall. Contests take place in a raised ring. A circulation space of at least 1.2 m must be provided between ring and spectator seating. Storage necessary for raised ring (if used) or floor mat, corner posts and ropes.

Specific lighting requirements – specialist advice should be obtained.

Fencing: the area (the piste) must be 1.8–2 m wide; the length is variable depending on the weapon used, with a minimum of 14 m. For two pistes and officials a space of at least 17 m × 8.6 m is required.
Can be in ancillary hall. If bleacher seating is used this should be set 2 m back from sides of piste. Storage required for mats.

Metal mats may be used for electrical scoring. If so, ring bolts will be required in floor to tension mats. Consult specialist fencing equipment sup-pliers.

Gymnastics: for both men's and women's competition a floor space of 32–36.5 m × 26 m and floor to ceiling height of 6.7–7.6 m is needed. A permanent area for gymnastics is desirable if at all possible. Equipment is large and cumbersome and much time and effort are saved if it is permanently installed. If main hall is used for teaching and practice and/or competitions a large storage area will be required.

A great deal of stress and strain is put on the apparatus during use – walls, ceiling and floor must be capable of supporting all weight-bearing equipment. Consult specialist gymnastics equip-ment suppliers.

Walls should be projection-free and non-abrasive.

Handball (seven-a-side): for competition play the court must be 30–40 m long by 20 m wide and 7.6–9 m high. Usual dimensions are 40 m × 20 m. For recreational play court can be 30 m × 17 m and 7.6 m high. On ends and one side 1 m clear space should be provided and 2 m on the other side to allow for substitutes, coaches, etc. Best viewing is from galleries but bleacher seating along sides – at least 2 m from side lines – is suitable. Storage necessary for portable goal-posts (can be dual-purpose with hockey).

Ideally, the pitch should be surrounded by portable 'walls' (side-boards) of 1.2 m min. height. Walls should be non-abrasive and without projections or indentations.

Hockey: ideal area is 40 m × 20 m but space can be 36 m × 18 m up to 44 m × 22 m. Clear space on sides 1.5 m and at ends 1.5–3 m. Best viewing is from galleries but bleacher seating all around pitch is suitable. Storage necessary for portable goal-posts (3.65 m wide × 1.83 m high) and portable walls if used.

No special requirements.

Judo: for international competitions the contest area (shiaijo) is 9 m square around which there is a 1 m danger area. This is surrounded by a safety area. The total space requirement is approximately 16 m × 16 m. Can be in ancillary hall. Storage necessary for mats which may be kept on trollies.

No special requirements.

Karate: a 6–10 m square area. A clear surround space of at least 1.5 m is required for officials, etc. Can be in ancillary hall.

No special requirements.

Kendo: area is usually 9–11 m × 11 m. A clear surround space of at least 1.5 m is required on three sides and 2.5 m on the other. Can be in ancillary hall.

No special requirements.

Lacrosse: for women's lacrosse a pitch of 29–42 m × 15–21 m. The men's game requires a pitch of 46–48 m × 18–24 m and thus an extra-large hall. At recreational level it can be played in a 36.5 m length. Storage necessary for goal-posts.

Court does not need to be enclosed but if it is there should be a space of 1.8 m all around and walls should be capable of acting as rebound surfaces.

Micro-korfball: minimum court size 27 m × 18 m (up to 60 m × 30 m). A clear space of at least 1.8–2 m is required all around court. The game is best viewed from galleries overlooking the court on both sides; bleacher seating on floor level is also suitable. Storage space of ±3.5 m high × 0.5 m × 0.5 m necessary for two goals.

Walls should be non-abrasive. Windows should be at least 2.4 m above floor level.

Netball: court size 30.5 m × 15.25 m × 7.6 m high. A clear space of at least 0.75–1.5 m should be provided around the court. Best spectator viewing is from sides. Storage of ±0.35 m^2 × 3 m high necessary for each goal.

If walls are used as boundaries they should be non-abrasive and without projections or indentations. Windows should not be lower than 3 m from floor level. Portable walls as for hockey.

Soccer (five-a-side): game can be adapted to the size of available space but minimum playing area should be 30 m × 18.5 m; maximum 36 m × 28 m. At recreational level 30 m × 15 m is acceptable. Best viewing is from gallery. Ideally there should be no free space around the pitch as a feature of the game is the use of walls as a rebound surface. If spectator seating is to be provided at floor level portable walls should be used. Storage of 6.5 m^2 × 1.2 m high for each set of portable goal-posts and for portable walls if used.

Table tennis: table is 2.74 m × 1.52 m. The overall space required varies depending on the level of play: recreational 7.6 m × 4.6 m; club tournaments 10 m × 5 m; county level 11–14 m × 5.5–7 m. For tournament play 7–9 tables can be accommodated in a 32 m × 17 m hall. Seating can be provided all around – best viewing is from sides. Storage necessary for tables.

Good artificial lighting is important and must be carefully planned – specialist advice should be obtained. Fluorescent tubes should be avoided. Service illuminance at table level should be between 150–400 lux. A draught-free atmosphere is required.

Tennis: size of court is 23.77 m × 10.97 m. A clear space of 3–4 m on each side and 5.5–6.4 m on each end is required. Height: for recreational play 7.6–8 m; for championship play 9 m. Spectator seating all around court with careful positioning at ends to avoid obscuring players' vision of ball. Storage necessary for net and posts, umpire's chair.

Walls should be without windows up to 3–4 m above floor level. Floor sockets may be required for fixing of posts.

Trampoline: size is 4.5–5.2 m × 2.7–3.05 m. A clear space of 3 m on each end and 2 m on the sides must be allowed for. Minimum floor to ceiling height 7 m. Storage necessary for trampoline(s) on roller stand(s), and safety nets.

A safety rig fixed to roof or ceiling is required over each trampoline for training. Specialist advice should be obtained.

Volleyball: court size is 18 m × 9 m. A clear surround space of 2–3 m is required. Seating can be provided all around the court. Storage necessary for the net (±1 m long × 300 mm in diameter when rolled up).

Hanging lights should be avoided as ball is constantly in the air. Players continually look upwards during play so the area must be glare-free.

Wrestling: size of mat depends on level of competition: international 12 m square; national, county or club 10–12 m square. For international competition a 3 m clear surround space is required while for national, county and club level 1–2 m is sufficient. Can be accommodated in ancillary hall. Storage necessary for mats.

No special requirements.

Projectile hall
A specialist hall for projectile sports is often provided in a multi-sports centre. It should be designed for maximum potential use so that its overall dimensions provide for maximum range of primary and secondary sports. Typical hall sizes in the UK:

Small   30.3 m × 5.3 m × 3.6 m high
Medium   30.3 m × 9.75 m × 3.6–4.6 m high
Large   30.3 m × 12.8 m × 4.6 m high

These are normally enclosed spaces not offering opportunities for casual viewing. Indirect access from foyer or other public space in a lobby (possibly with glazed screen) is advisable; this provides a security zone and acoustic barrier. Club room(s) (possibly with viewing windows) can be part of lobby or lead off from it. Decide on sports to be accommodated. Prepare list of equipment required by each activity. Determine method of fixing and storing all equipment.

Careful design is required to ensure a pleasant atmosphere in this enclosed space. Construction and finishes must be robust.
Requirements for floor will vary according to sports accommodated: properly sealed granolithic flooring may be suitable.
A good, even level of glare-free artificial lighting (approximately 350 lux) will be required throughout the hall with special lighting for targets (archery and shooting).
Sound-absorbent materials should be included on ceilings, upper walls and other areas where compatible with use. Determine requirements for and system of ventilation and heating.

Sports types
All of the following, with the exception of shooting, could be included in the main hall. The nature of the area required, however, may rule out concurrent use of the hall.

e-standing backstop may be required behind targets and should be of the same material as gets; soft and resilient so as not to damage the arrow heads.

Archery: competition distances are 30 m, 25 m or 18 m (also 20 yards = 18.288 m). For club and recreational purposes 15 yards (13.716 m) is acceptable. Distance from side wall to target should be at least 1.2 m, and from back wall to target 2 m. Archers stand at least 1.25 m apart on shooting line with two or three to each target. Waiting line is 5 m behind shooting line.

Two targets with two archers to each can be placed in width of 5 m, three archers to each in width of 7.5 m. Allow for spectators, seated or standing (if required) behind archers. Storage necessary for targets, straw bosses, stands and backstop.

No other special requirements.

Bowls: recreational play can be provided on a temporary basis by use of 'roll-out' carpets or on a permanent basis in a purpose-designed area (see 'Specialist facilities' below). Roll-out rinks should each be 4.55 m wide by a minimum of 32 m long (full length is 37.49 m).

End 'ditches' have to be provided. These may be in the form of a 300 mm × 200 mm recess in the floor covered with a hinged cover plate. Storage necessary for mats.

Natural lighting from above (clerestory). Artificial lighting should be at least 4.5 m from the floor and shielded from the eyes of the batsmen. Tracking on the ceiling will be required for suspending nets.

Cricket practice: nets require length of 30.5–33.5 m and width of 3.05–3.65 m. One version of six-a-side cricket is played in three adjacent nets. The normal game requires a playing area of 30.4–36.5 m × 18.9–30.4 m × 6.1–7.6 m high.

A solid rather than suspended floor is considered best. Mats for batsmen and bowlers are laid on top of floor. Provision must be made for hanging vertical nets to enclose pitches and a horizontal net over pitches. Storage necessary for mats, netting and wickets.

No special requirements.

Golf practice: driving is practised in a 'range' with netting (18 mm mesh) on three sides and below the ceiling. A space of 6.7 m × 2.4 m plus surrounds is sufficient. The same area can be used for putting which is practised on a roll-out carpet. Storage necessary for mats and netting.

For details see 'Specialist facilities' below.

Shooting: this may be practised in projectile hall but a separate specialist range is best as lead pollution can be a problem.

SPECIALIST FACILITIES

Floor must be stable and level and usually consists of screeded concrete covered with felt or jute laid transversely on a felt underlay; an alternative finish is nylon-based carpeting. Carpet must be laid at right angles to direction of play. The floor construction and finish is important to ensure a good playing surface and should be discussed with the manufacturer of the selected finish.

Ditches should be 38–200 mm deep; the base should contain some soft material to prevent damage to woods.

No direct sunlight should be allowed to fall onto the green. If natural lighting is used illumination should be even and glare avoided. Artificial lighting from above – 300 lux horizontally on the green.

Bowls: an indoor bowling-green does not have to be square: play is in one direction only because of the seams in the carpet. The green is divided into rinks each of which should have the following dimensions:

Length   36.5 m (min 34.75 m; max 40 m)
Width   4.8 m (min 4.5 m ; max 5.4 m)

– the two outside rinks should be 300 mm wider than the inside rinks.

Additional space is required in the form of a ditch around the rink 200–375 mm wide (100–200 mm deep) at the ends and 125 mm wide (38–200 mm deep) at the sides. A bank and surround of at least 1.5 m must be provided all around.

The number of rinks is determined by standard of play and estimated demand from catchment area which may be larger than for other indoor sports: one rink per 14,000–17,000 of the total population or 6,200–7,400 of population aged 45 years and over.

For district and local championships a minimum of four greens must be provided. Bowling greens are used by the physically disabled and must be designed with them in mind. Surrounds may have to be wider than 1.5 m to allow space for spectator seating. Bowlers may use the general facilities for changing, but simple separate facilities ($\pm$ 5 m^2 per rink for males and females) and toilets are often provided. Benches, coat hooks (eight per rink), a mirror and small lockers (one per member) to take bowls and shoes should be included.

A refreshment area should be located adjacent to the green. A club room, a small office and a reception/control area may be required. Storage necessary for chairs or other spectator seating, scoreboards, vacuum cleaner and other equipment.

Climbing-walls: these are a potentially dangerous but popular facility if well designed. They should, however, only be included if there is a definite need or demand. The advice of an official mountain climbing organisation must be obtained: discuss the details (including location, height and length) of the proposed wall.

Height is usually at least 5 m; for schools and youth clubs, 3.5 m is adequate. There must be sufficient space at the wall base for instructors and other people to stand.

Degree of difficulty of design will depend on standard of climbers it is intended for. The wall should not be in too prominent a position nor be located too close to other activity areas. Ideally the wall should not, therefore, be in the main hall; the ancillary hall is a possibility but height may be a problem. There should be no projections from the wall lower than 2 m above the floor.

Walls can be monolithic – built of natural rock (both boulders and cut rock) or concrete cast to simulate rock – or of brickwork with various features, usually of precast concrete, built in. Prefabricated units of concrete or fibre glass are also a possibility. Monolithic walls are usually too massive for indoor locations.

Ice-skating rink: the majority of these are used for general recreational skating, figure-skating, ice-dancing, ice-hockey, curling and speed-skating. The size of an all-purpose rink is normally determined by requirements for ice-hockey (minimum 56 m $\times$ 26 m – corners 7 m radius, maximum 61 m $\times$ 30 m – corners 8.5 m radius), as this is suitable for other activities. Rinks to be used for recreational skating only should allow approximately 2.5 m^2–4 m^2 per person; this type of rink can be circular in shape. Space will have to be provided for a skate hire shop and repair shop. If the rink is operated as an independent entity, reception area, offices and changing-rooms will have to be included. A control room for public address/music may be required.

For ice-hockey the rink should be surrounded by a solid continuous fence known as 'the boards' – height 1 m minimum and 1.22 m maximum – with suitably positioned access/exit points for skaters and a 3 m-wide gate for the ice re-surfacing machine. Gates must open away from the ice surface. A circulation space of at least 1.2 m–1.5 m must be provided around the perimeter. A 3 m $\times$ 1.8 m $\times$ 1.8 m deep snow pit is usually required at edge of rink and below rink level; the technical requirements for this pit will have to be determined.

Floor construction is very important and specialist advice should be obtained. Heaving of the floor due to freezing and expansion of the soil under the rink are problems – ground and ground water conditions must be checked. Drainage and/or heating of the sub-soil may be required. The construction consists basically of: concrete base slab (may contain heating for sub-soil); insulation (usually in two layers); damp-proof membrane; concrete or sand bed containing the refrigeration pipes. Synthetic ice surfaces suitable for recreational skating are available. Obtain advice on refrigeration from specialist consultant to determine system (direct or indirect), type of plant and pipes, etc. Plant room will need to be approximately 11 m $\times$ 6 m $\times$ 3.7 m high.

It is recommended that the temperature be maintained at around 10–13°C. Heating/cooling combined with mechanical ventilation is most common; warm air must not be circulated directly above ice surface. Consider recycling heat generated by the refrigeration plant and rejected at the condenser.

Lighting should be flexible so that it may be altered to suit different activities. Intensity from 300 lux (recreational) to 500 lux (club standard) horizontal on rink. No direct sunlight should fall onto the ice surface.

Walls and ceilings should be designed to reduce noise reverberation.

Storage necessary for goal-posts (1.22 m high × 1.83 m wide × 1 m deep), linemarking machine and resurfacing machine (size must be checked; ensure direct, clear access from store to rink). Bleacher seating may have to be stored.

No other specialist requirements.

Rowing tanks: this type of training facility simulates actual rowing conditions and is often included in or linked to the swimming-pool hall. An area of approximately 13 m–18 m × 9 m is required. A specially constructed tank and 'boat' are necessary. Specialist advice must be obtained.

Internal projections must be avoided. Walls and ceilings must be bullet-proof and any surface or element likely to result in backsplash (ricochet of stray bullets) should be lined with timber (minimum thickness 25 mm). Specialist advice should be obtained.
Walls and ceilings should also be sound-absorbent to reduce reverberation.
A bullet-proof backstop (or bullet catcher) and target mount is required. There are various systems; get specialist advice.
An air exhaust system – separate from general ventilation provision of centre – must be provided to exhaust combustion gases and lead dust; inlet at firing end, outlet at target end; discharged air should be filtered.
Good overall lighting is required (150 lux with 300 lux on and behind the firing line). Targets must be evenly illuminated (1,000 lux) from above or, preferably, below.

Shooting: if certain precautions are taken the projectile hall may be used. The maximum indoor shooting range is normally 25 m. The space should be at least 30.3 m long to allow for bullet stop behind the target and an assembly and spectator area behind the firing line. The width can vary depending on the number of firing points provided (for pistol 1.2 m and for rifle 1.8 m width per firing point).
A club room may be required with space for cupboards (for special clothing, targets, shooting mats, etc.), and for cleaning and repairing guns, as well as an armoury – either a walk-in cupboard with steel cabinets or a series of separate cells. Special permission (in the UK from the Ministry of Defence and police) may be required. Information can be obtained from the local authority or the appropriate shooting associations. Assembly and spectator area should be separated from firing area by at least a rail. A waist-high partition with glass above reduces possible disturbance to participants.
Some type of target transport system may be required – the most expensive is a completely automatic electrical one.

The wall surface is very important. It must be true, hard, smooth, plumb, coloured white, able to withstand impact and to absorb a certain amount of condensation. Most common construction is plastered brickwork finished with special squash court paint. There are various alternatives including one-way glass on up to three sides. Specialist advice should be obtained.
Floor must be hard, smooth, true, non-slip, light in colour and able to absorb moisture. A slightly sprung timber floor is best; boards must be laid parallel to side walls. Playboard or 'tin' must extend right across bottom of front wall 483 mm high, of metal or metal-faced plywood.
Walls above playing area and the ceiling should be of sound-absorbent material to reduce reverberation.
Good ventilation is essential; extractor fans may be required.
Artificial lighting, providing an even intensity of ± 380 lux at 1 m above floor level is best. Glare and shadows must be avoided.

Squash: in the UK provision is based on at least one court per 1,500 of population in catchment area, or 100–120 members (maximum) per court for clubs. Local competition normally requires two or three courts. Court size: 9.754 m × 6.4 m × 5.4 m–5.8 m high. The American court is 9.75 m × 5.64 m × 4.88 m high. Additional space may be required for spectators behind the court (if glass back wall is used) or on gallery.
There are cost advantages in siting courts side by side with common 'party walls' and a continuous linear gallery for spectators.
Squash courts generate a great deal of noise; keep this in mind when deciding on their situation within the centre.
The door to the court must be centrally placed in the back wall, set flush with the plaster and with no protrusions.
For match play there should be provision for a referee to stand above the centre of the back wall with an unobstructed view of the court.

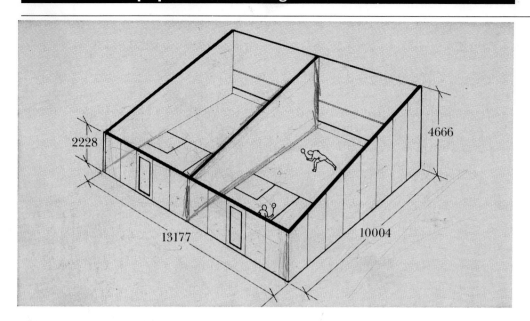

Fig. 2.13 *There are various forms of proprietary prefabricated squash courts ranging from complete buildings to units designed to fit within an 'umbrella' building. The example illustrated here is of the latter type with walls constructed from precast concrete panels which require no finish other than paint. (From leaflet of Banbury Squash Courts Ltd.).*

Fig. 2.14 *The patented 'Courtback' seating system used where squash courts are in back-to-back arrangements with a conventional glass wall on one court and the 'Courtback' system forming the wall of the court opposite. When required, up to 122 tiered seating places can be provided by extending the seating into the auditorium court. (From brochure of Audience Systems Ltd.).*

Fig. 2.15 *Squash court dimensions – the width and length of the court are given between finished wall faces. Rear wall can be solid or of glass at least 2.134 m high.*

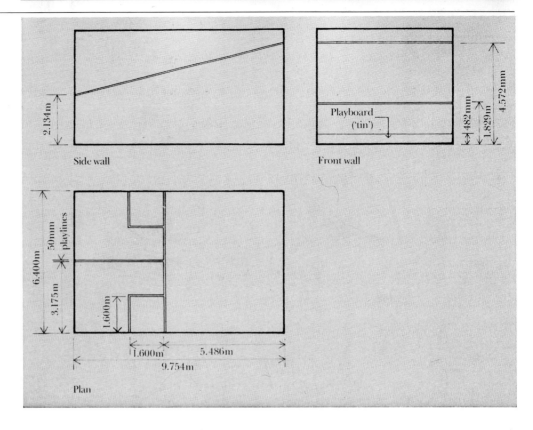

The floor of the bowlers' seating and other areas behind the lane installation should be raised 0.33 m above the concrete floor of the lanes area. For details of lanes and equipment consult specialist manufacturer/supplier.

Tenpin bowling: the overall length of the bowling lanes including the approach area and the automatic pinsetter is 25–25.5 m depending on the type of automatic equipment used. A clear service passage – minimum 914 mm, preferably 1.5–1.8 m – must be provided behind the lanes and a bowlers' seating area of 3.0–3.5 m in front of the lanes.

The width required depends on the number of lanes to be included: two lanes, 3.46 m; four lanes, 6.85 m; six lanes, 10.23 m. For each additional pair of lanes add 3.387 m. Side (or access) aisles must connect the concourse area to the service passage (minimum width 0.76 m).

Additional space may be required for a concourse area behind the players' seating, spectator seating, a control counter and manager's office. Spectator seating is usually provided between the bowlers' seating and the concourse.

The bowling alley must be linked to (or provided with) locker area and toilets and refreshment facilities. Facilities are roughly calculated on the basis of five persons per lane. Storage necessary for pins, pinsetter parts, etc., together with a small workshop either behind or to the side of the lanes.

Ceiling, walls and floor must be structurally strong enough to support heavy equipment, some of which may be strenuously used. Foam-backed PVC carpet or rubber tiling are commonly used for flooring.
Good ventilation is required.

Weight-training: normally requires a self-contained space in which equipment is permanently installed as it is impracticable to move it from place to place. Space can range from between 80 m to 148 m^2: a space 10 m–12 m^2 × 3.5 m high is adequate. If majority of equipment is loose and movable, space could be used for boxing training. Must be accessible to changing-rooms and, if possible, the sauna. Determine what equipment is to be provided and fixing requirements. If multi-station exercisers are to be used, determine space requirements from manufacturer.

The activities can be noisy; this may be a problem particularly if room is located over other spaces.

Storage necessary for canvas mat, ropes, ring posts, boxing gloves, etc., if space is also used for boxing.

2 Indoor games and general activities

Arts workshop

A space of 9–15 m^2 with height of approximately 4.5 m would be suitable for drama workshops, music practice and recitals and as an exhibition space. An ancillary/practice hall (see 2.25.1) could be used for this purpose. The room should ideally be close to the refreshment and public toilet facilities and to the changing-rooms. The following would be useful:

— a small projection booth which could double as a control room for sound and lighting.
— a gallery for seating and access to lighting – alternatively a catwalk.
— a large external door for bringing in scenery and other equipment.

Storage necessary for the various possible pieces of equipment used in the space: piano, audio, seating, tables, platforms, costumes, etc. An area of 50 m^2 or more may be required.

A grid for flexible artificial lighting should be provided over the whole area. Windows should be kept small and be fitted with blackout blinds. A semi-sprung wooden floor would be ideal. A continuous curtain track should be provided around the perimeter of the space. If the room is to be used for movement and dance, mirrors and barres will be required (see 'Dancing' below).

The acoustics of the space will need special consideration.

Billiards/snooker

Because of size and weight (about 27 kg) of table it cannot be moved easily and a separate space should be provided for it. Overall size of table 3.7–4 m × 1.9–2 m. Clear playing space around table 1.7–2 m. Minimum area required, excluding seating, 7 × 5.25 m. Minimum space between tables: end to end 2.25 m; side to side 3.2 m.

A bay off a multi-purpose room could be used. If two tables are to be included they are best installed end to end. Spectator seating can be provided all around the table or on three sides of each table in a two-table space.

Storage is not normally required.

Since the table must be plumbed and accurately levelled a firm level floor is required. Vinyl tiles are commonly used for floor covering; carpeting tends to wear out quickly. Canopy fitting lighting – to take three 100 or 150 watt tungsten filament lamps – is usually suspended centrally above table. Specialist should be consulted. Metered lighting may be required.

Good ventilation is essential.

Committee/club room(s)

This must usually accommodate a great many different activities including group and table games. To determine requirements list main anticipated uses. The space may also be put to certain special uses (see 2.25.3). The space should measure at least 8 m × 4.5 m.

The room should ideally be close to the refreshment and public toilet facilities. Where two or more rooms are provided, sliding folding acoustic room dividers – allowing individual rooms to be combined – will provide more flexibility. Freedom from outside noise is important.

A flexible lighting system (with maximum level approximately 300 lux) is preferable. Windows should be fitted with blackout blinds. Pinning boards and a blackboard should be provided. A sink with drainer will increase flexibility of the space (can also be used for handicrafts).

Storage depends on the needs of the individual activities to be accommodated but provision should be generous for, among other things, tables, chairs and portable platforms.

Dancing

Determine heating, ventilation and lighting requirements of local licensing authority at an early stage. Lighting should be flexible enough to create the correct atmosphere for different occasions, for example, cabaret.

A semi-sprung wooden floor is ideal: hardwood strips fixed to softwood battens. Boards should be laid so that dancing is predominantly in the direction of the grain (this adds to the life of the floor).

Acoustic treatment of the ceiling will probably be necessary.

Establish whether dancing is to be the primary activity and what other purposes the space will be used for. The arts workshop or an ancillary/practice hall (see 2.25.1) could be used for this purpose. As a general guide allow $0.56\,m^2$ of floor space per dancer. Check with relevant local licensing authority to ensure that it also bases its calculation on this figure. Where dancing is the primary activity the width of the dancing area should be a minimum of 10.5 m. Length preferably 2–2½ times width. Rostrum for six-piece band requires $12\,m^2$; nine-piece band $16\,m^2$.

The room should ideally be close to the refreshment and public toilet facilities. For best projection of the music, the band should be located centrally on one of the longer sides of the dancing area. Rostrum should be so shaped as to minimise the risk of dancers bumping into it. Storage may be required for movable rostrum, tables and chairs.

Darts

Walls on which the boards are to be hung should be faced with panels of fibreboard or other similar material. Each board should be lit by an adjustable spotlight suspended from the ceiling.

Could be played in multi-purpose space that is used for other activities when darts is not being played. Projectile hall could be used (see 2.25.1). Throwing lanes for each board 3.0–3.66 m × 1.8–2.4 m. For boards placed side-to-side, 1.5 m must be allowed between throwing lanes. Allow minimum of 2 m between back of lanes and any seating. Boards should not be placed adjacent to doors. Spectator seating can be allowed for behind the throwing space.

Storage necessary for dart boards and floor mats.

Groups and table games

A sound-absorbent ceiling is desirable. Good, even, natural and artificial lighting should be provided. Illumination level on table should be at least 200 lux.

Group games such as bingo and beetle drives, and table games (cards, chess, etc.) can be played in a multi-purpose space which could also be used for dancing or group cultural activities. To calculate area required allow a space of 2.4 m × 2.4 m per table and four chairs.

The room should ideally be close to the refreshment and public toilet facilities.

Storage necessary for tables and chairs, and for games (possibly in cupboard).

Movement and dance

Lighting should be warm and flexible (dimmers and part switching) to help create different moods. General level at floor of 200 lux.

A semi-sprung wooden floor is ideal.

Barres should be mounted on two walls at heights of 0.914 m and 1.067 m. Wall-mounted mirrors 2 m plus high and 450–600 mm above floor should be as wide as possible. A pinning board and a blackboard should be provided.

A space of 15–17 m × 12–17 m with a minimum floor to ceiling height of 4.5 m is recommended for this popular form of physical recreation. A space of 9 m × 9 m can be used by small practice groups. The arts workshop or an ancillary/practice hall (see 2.25.1) could be used. A large hall can be subdivided by partitions or curtains but noise between the areas could be a problem. The room should ideally be close to the changing-rooms.

A congenial atmosphere must be created: the space should have relatively large, curtained windows to give natural light, ventilation and a pleasant view to outdoors.

Storage will be necessary for audio equipment on rollaway fitting, piano, movable platform, chairs and possibly portable barres, mirrors, etc.

Sauna suite

If a sauna suite is a separate entity the following will be required in addition to the hot room: reception/staff area, changing area with clothes storage, wash area, lounge/rest area. The suite can, however, be part of the main changing/shower complex.

Depending on layout each bather will occupy 3–5 m^2 at any one time and this figure can be used to work out total capacity of the suite. A sauna of approximately 2.5 m × 3.2 m will seat eight bathers; one of 3.2 m × 3.8 m, about 11 bathers. Floor to ceiling height approximately 2.8 m. Massage cubicles (each approximately 2.8 m × 2.2 m) are often included. If separate facilities are provided for males and

Specialist advice should be obtained concerning sauna construction/heating. Ventilation of the sauna is very important, as is the positioning of the inlet and outlet openings to ensure correct air-flow. Specialist advice should be obtained. Strong electric lighting can mar the tranquil atmosphere of the sauna. The light must be indirect and the fittings unobtrusive, preferably above or slightly behind the bathers' normal field of vision.

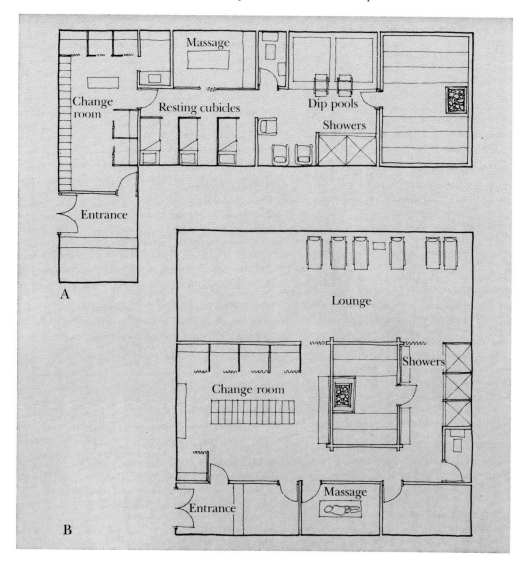

Fig. 2.16 *Alternative layout for large sauna installations, A: straight-through layout, and B: circular system. Separate facilities are usually provided for males and females, sometimes with a common reception area. The alternative is to have one installation with sessions allotted to each sex.*

Fig. 2.17   *In a large sauna, the layout of the benches provides more flexibility of use and does not restrict the plan dimension of the room as in a smaller sauna. Numbers 1–3 show platform arrangements and number 4 a layout with parallel benches.*

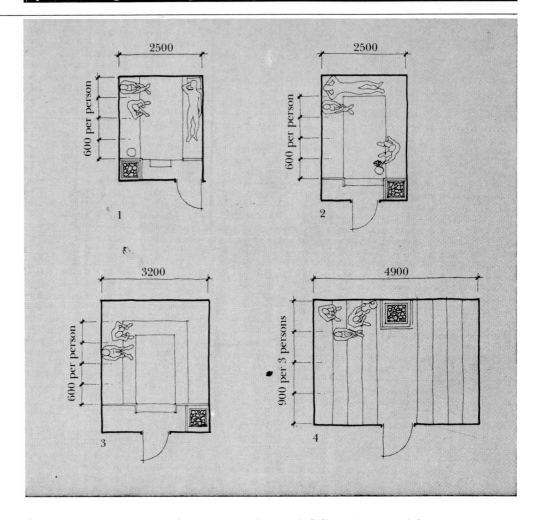

females a common reception area can be used. When space and finance permit it, two smaller sauna rooms maintained at different temperatures would be better than one large room.

The wet area – showers and possibly plunge pool – should be at least equal to area of sauna(s); the rest area (with refreshment facilities), about three or four times the sauna area.

Storage of towels and robes may be necessary at or near the reception area.

Solarium

Main considerations are space and power requirements of solarium equipment. Consult manufacturers/suppliers.

Area required will depend on number of units provided and type of equipment used. As a general guide allow approximately 6 m² per tanning 'station' including circulation space. Solarium could be part of sauna suite: part of or linked to rest area or part of main swimming-pool complex.

Workshop

Good natural lighting to be free from glare;

A multi-purpose craft area can be used for basket-making, pottery, model-making,

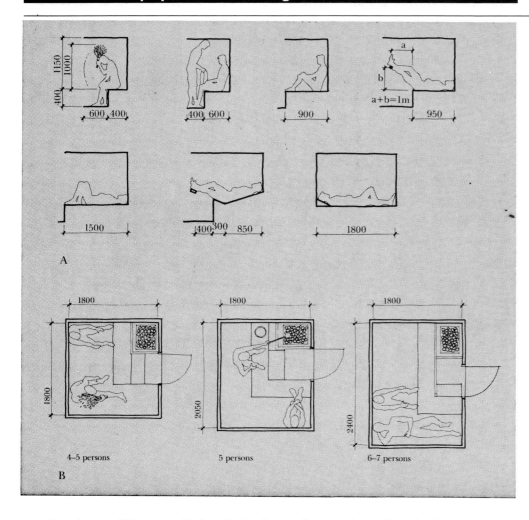

Fig. 2.18.
A: *the width and shape of the sauna bench or platform varies according to the way in which it will be used.*
B: *typical layout and sizes of smaller saunas.*

woodwork, etc. The overall size depends on the number of work places and the activities to be provided for. If fixed perimeter work benches and movable free-standing benches are provided, a space of approximately 6.7 m square will be required; for six free-standing benches, 6.7 m × 9.6 m.

As this space is likely to generate considerable noise, care must be taken with its siting relative to the other elements in the complex.

Supervision may be a problem in a large centre.

An outside door for delivery of materials should be provided.

Storage (possibly with direct external access) necessary for materials (timber, clay, etc.) and tools. Also possibly for movable work benches when clear floor space is needed in workshop, for example when building scenery for amateur dramatics presentation.

3 Special uses

Some of the sports or recreational spaces may occasionally be used for various special community activities. A brief summary of the main requirements for the

artificial lighting (usually fluorescent) at a level of 200–250 lux.

Determine what machinery/electrical equipment is to be used: three-phase power supply may be needed.

Choose simple finishes, robust and easy to clean. Ceilings should be sound absorbent to reduce noise levels.

more common activities is given so that client and architect can assess approximately what will be involved.

Blood donation centre

Establish number and flow of donors to be catered for. Each team of workers will require twelve beds: six for bleeding, six for resting. Each group of six beds will require an area of 37–56 m²; a reception area of approximately 14 m² should be provided. Tea-making facilities must be available and storage for beds may be required. The centre should preferably be at ground-floor level and with easy access from a road or car park for unloading equipment.

Civil defence

Requirements include lecture room seating about 50 people with facilities for film and slide projection, a smaller room seating 25, one or two rooms each accommodating 15, and a main assembly area for social occasions and special meetings – refreshment and bar areas would be used for these functions.

Fashion shows and beauty contests

In one of the main halls banked seating should be arranged, if possible, in a horseshoe shape around a raised display walkway 762 mm high × 914 mm wide minimum. Space for changing and for storage of clothes will also be required.

Polling centre

The room used should be at ground level and able to be reached without steps – to cater for the elderly and physically handicapped – and have separate entrance and exit doors. Space must be large enough to provide one booth measuring 762 mm wide × 2,134 mm high, for every 150 people on the electoral roll using that particular centre.

Boy Scouts, Girl Guides and other youth organisations

For Scout and Guide activities a space 9–14 m long × 6–7.5 m wide is desirable. At least four separate spaces – which may be formed with removable partitions – each approximately 1.5 m × 1.8 m, are required around the main space. A simple kitchen of 7–9 m² and storage space are required. Other youth organisations have similar needs.

4 Administrative, refreshment, social and ancillary areas

Entrance hall/control area

Space must be large enough to accommodate normal flow of public – participants and spectators – with area for waiting (including some seats). Consideration must be given to crowds leaving main activity areas after spectator events or special functions. Minimum area to be approximately $20\,m^2$. Reception/control space is usually glass-enclosed for security and large enough to accommodate two people; minimum area around $10\,m^2$. If automatic ticket machines and turnstiles are to be used, space requirements should be obtained from manufacturers/suppliers. If cloakroom area – for temporary storage of spectators' overcoats and umbrellas – is required, allow $0.1\,m^2$ per person.

Consider undercover provision for people having to queue at times. There must be access from entrance hall to shops (where applicable), public telephones and toilets, refreshment areas, changing rooms, etc. Consider segregation of players and spectators where required (as in pool hall). Reception/control office staff should have good view of major circulation spaces and vending machines for supervision, and space must be positioned so that all users must pass it to enter activity areas. It must, therefore, be in a prominent position.

Consider directional signs and possible planting.

Reception/control office will require microphone for public address system; internal and external telephones; also possibly TV monitors for supervision of certain areas. Sufficient counter space must be provided for this equipment as well as cash register, booking sheets, etc. A small safe may be required.

Provide recess for vending machines if possible; provision is required for water and electrical services; also for waste bins and storage.

Finishes should be both attractive and durable. Flooring must be non-slip, easily cleaned and not show dirt. A generous area of door matting must be provided.

Office(s)

The types, sizes and number of offices depend upon the size of centre, number of staff, managerial policy and organisation. A rough guide of likely minimum areas is: manager's office $14–20\,m^2$; general offices (supervisor, engineer, instructors/coaches, etc.) $9–11\,m^2$; secretary/typist $8–9\,m^2$.

Offices should, ideally, be close to reception/control space but away from main public circulation areas. Group offices should be together as far as possible. Some (instructors/coaches) may need to be adjacent to activity areas or changing-rooms.

No special requirements. Advice may be obtained from the Institute of Baths and Recreation Management and the Institute of Leisure and Amenity Management – see Appendix A.1.

Staff restroom, changing-room and toilets

Sizes will depend on the number of staff. Area of $10–15\,m^2$ will probably be required for restroom. Changing and toilet facilities may be separate for males and females or shared. One WC and one wash-basin will be adequate for up to 15 persons.

The restroom should be sited in a quiet area of building adjacent to changing-room and toilets, and with easy access to offices. Instructors/coaches may need separate changing, locker and shower facilities.

A sink and electrical outlet should be provided in restroom for tea-making. Lockers may be required in changing-room.

Refreshment and social facilities

Bar: to determine overall (customer and servery) space required allow approximately $0.6\,m^2$ per person if only drink is served; where food is also served, $0.9\,m^2$ per person. The average bar area is around $140–150\,m^2$. Storage space (excluding empties) of between $75–100\,m^2$ will be required.

Restaurant/cafeteria: with seating at tables for four-six people (self-service or table service) allow 0.9–1.4 m² per person. Additional space may be required for either a snack bar or vending machines to serve bathers using the pool area.

The refreshment areas should, ideally, be sited at the heart of the centre, possibly overlooking the major activity areas and, if possible, should be visible from the entrance hall.

Public toilets must be situated adjacent to the refreshment areas. The bar should be linked to the kitchen and storage areas. Storage for beer should be either directly below or directly adjacent to the servery; store for wine, spirits and tobacco must be lockable as well as accessible for deliveries.

In a complex with leisure-type pool, the restaurant may have to be accessible to bathers and spectators from the pool surround.

Kitchen: the area required will depend on type and number of meals to be served at peak periods. As an approximate guide the ratio of dining to kitchen area will vary between 3:1 (for only one sitting) and 1:1 where there are two or more sittings per meal. Space may be required for catering manager's office: staff rest area, toilet, etc.

Kitchen must have direct access to both restaurant/cafeteria and bar. Specialist advice should be obtained on kitchen layout and storage (cold stores, dry stores, etc.) requirements. An enclosed yard for refuse bins, storage of crates and empty bottles will be needed.

Toilets: statutory requirements vary from place to place. A general guide is:

Men   WCs: minimum two (up to 200 persons), then one for each 100 up to 500, then one for each additional 200.
        Urinals: minimum two (up to 1,000), then one for each 50.
        Wash-basins: one for each 60.
Women WCs: minimum two (up to 75), then one for each 50.
        Wash-basins: one for each 60 persons.

At least one compartment (1.5 m × 2 m) must be provided for wheelchair users. Toilets must be close to both entrance hall and the refreshment areas. They should be laid out so that whole space can be seen on entering.

Crèche: a separate space may be required. Alternatively a committee/club room (used mainly during the evenings) may be used as a crèche during the day. At least 2.5 m² per child should be allowed. This does not include toilets: one WC and one wash-basin should be provided per every 12 children. In addition a refreshment area may be necessary. Windows should, if possible, be low enough for children to see out of. Plenty of pinning board should be provided on the walls. Adequate storage is needed for tables, chairs, play mats, toys, etc.

Finishes and design should help to create a warm, informal and relaxed atmosphere: heavy-duty carpet tiles on floor can contribute towards this and help to reduce noise levels. Lighting must also help to create correct atmosphere; level required is around 150 lux.
Sufficient counter and back fittings must be provided for the bar servery (consult specialist bar fitters for detailed information) including a double sink for glass washing with drinking-water supply.
A staff wash-basin must be readily accessible from the servery area.

For more detailed information see Appendix A.1.b: *New Metric Handbook*[11], chapter 20 and Lawson[18].
Lighting: level required around 500 lux. Ventilation: rate must be at least 20 air changes per hour. For detailed information and advice on equipment and fittings consult specialist manufacturer/supplier.

Finishes must be hard-wearing, impervious, easy to clean and vandal-proof. Fittings must be robust and vandal-proof; care must be taken with detailing. See also 'Changing-rooms' below.

Toilets, wash-basins and coat hooks must all be at low level. Ceiling should be of sound-absorbent material. Maximum general lighting level required is 200 lux.

Changing-rooms

The number of changing-spaces should relate to the maximum utilisation of the facilities with allowance for overlap. For dry sports calculate maximum number of persons using each activity space during a one hour period and double total to allow for overlap. For swimming-pools changing-space is normally related to pool area: one place for each $8.4\,m^2$ of water area ($6.5\,m^2$ in the case of leisure pools) plus one place for each $4.2\,m^2$ of learner pool area. Add two places for a diving pool. Area required is generally based on $0.7–0.85\,m^2$ per person which includes 400–500 mm of bench space per person.

Provision should be made for a drying/towelling area between the showers and changing-spaces.

Changing-rooms must be centrally placed in the complex particularly if they are shared by swimming-pool(s) and dry sports. Changing can be all cubicles, open plan or (most commonly) a combination of the two. In this case space mainly for open changing with some cubicles provided for the shy (minimum size 800 mm $\times$ 900 mm: 1 m $\times$ 1 m preferred) and for the disabled (2 m $\times$ 2 m) which can double for family use. The proportion of cubicles to open changing-area may need to be increased for females. It is important for the layout to achieve maximum flexibility with minimum supervision. Interchange rooms can be considered. If interchange rooms are provided these can be used for sports teams and locked for clothes storage. This, however, restricts use of space by other people. If a clothes storage system is used, consider combined store (serving both male and female areas) as this will save on staff. Full-sized lockers are approximately 0.5 m $\times$ 0.5 m; some larger lockers may be needed for participants in dry sports.

Clothes storage: either in individual lockers – which can be grouped together or dispersed – or in central store (for hangers/baskets). Both systems require approximately the same area. For dry sports, storage space (usually lockers) should be provided for the estimated number of players using the facilities per hour $\times$ 2.5, while for swimmers, storage units for 4–6 times the number of changing-places are normally provided.

Showers (pre-cleanse) and toilets: provision is based on the number of changing-places provided.

WCs (2 minimum)	1 per 15–20 (males); 1 per 7–10 (females)
Urinals	1 per 15–20
Showers	1 per 7–8 both males and females
Wash-basins	1 per 15 both males and females

At least one cubicle for use by the disabled.

Showers and toilets must be placed so that bathers pass them on their way to the pool. Stairs and steps must be avoided. Access to pool from this area to be at shallow end. A small warm room (temperature 30–40°C; on the Continent up to 50–55°C) is sometimes provided between the shower area and pool. The sauna is often planned in conjunction with the pre-cleanse area.

Finishes should offer maximum durability with minimum maintenance: hard-wearing, impervious, corrosion-resistant, and easily washable. Flooring should be non-slip even when wet (grooved, fully vitrified ceramic tiles); to facilitate hosing down it should have minimum slope of 1:24 away from cubicles, lockers, etc. to drains. PVC duckboards can be used in drying area. Walls in shower area should be fully tiled.

Cubicles, lockers, benches and other fixtures and fittings must be robust and vandal-proof: screws, pipework and WC cisterns should be concealed; light fittings should be recessed; coat hooks should be short; curtain rail should be sturdy and securely fixed; fit theft-proof plugs to wash-basins and recessed soap holders.

Shower heads to be 1.67 m above the floor for males and 1.5 m for females. At least one unit should have a seat and flexible lead connection for the disabled. Water supply system must allow for all showers to operate simultaneously. Hose points must be provided for washing of floors.

There should be at least one full-length mirror (or horizontal mirror behind vanity top) in each changing-room. Coin-operated hair dryers (wall mounted) may be required. Because of the humid atmosphere, good ventilation – 8 to 10 air changes per hour – is essential.

Fig. 2.19 *Basic layout of changing-facilities.*

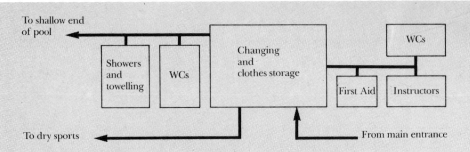

A Main elements of changing facilities (Note : separate change facilities are sometimes provided for wet and dry sports)

B. Change areas: where individual lockers are used these may be in a separate space – sometimes shared by males and females – or in the change room itself

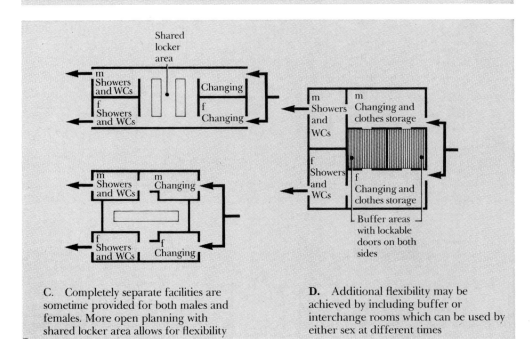

C. Completely separate facilities are sometime provided for both males and females. More open planning with shared locker area allows for flexibility

D. Additional flexibility may be achieved by including buffer or interchange rooms which can be used by either sex at different times

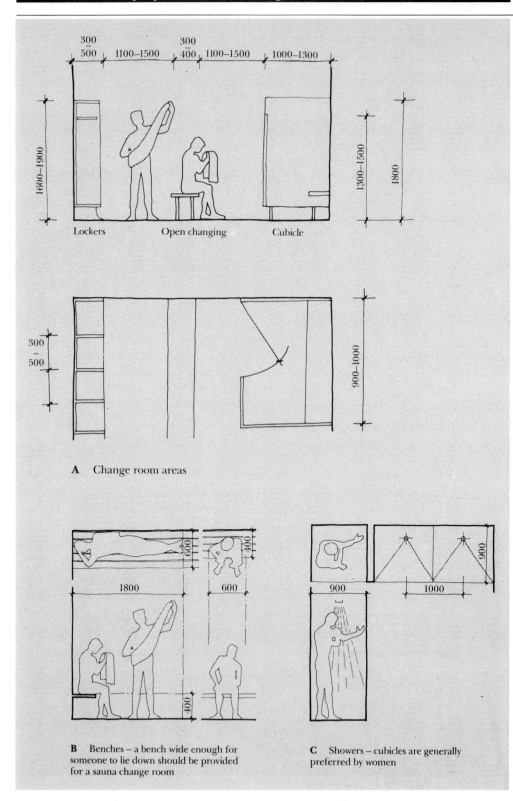

Fig. 2.20 *Change-rooms and showers, some basic dimensions.*

Lockers   Open changing   Cubicle

A Change room areas

B Benches – a bench wide enough for someone to lie down should be provided for a sauna change room

C Showers – cubicles are generally preferred by women

An open shower area is acceptable for males; for females separate shower cubicles should be provided.

First-aid room

Finishes to be impervious and easily cleanable. A sink with hot and cold water supply and a cupboard for storage of blankets, first-aid material, oxygen cylinder, etc., is required.

Minimum area required is 9–10 m^2. It must be accessible from all main outdoor spaces and have direct external access for ambulances. Doors should be minimum 1.07 m wide to allow passage of stretchers.

Storage areas

Sliding or up-and-over doors are commonly used for storage areas. Doors and fittings should be flush with adjoining wall surfaces in sports halls (no projections) and strong enough to withstand impact. Cleaner's store may require sink with drainer and hot and cold water.

Further storage areas may be necessary in addition to the specialised storage areas already described. It is difficult to generalise, and only a rough guide to areas can be given. For example, poolside storage (can also be adjacent to pool hall) may be required for lines, starting-blocks, waterpolo nets, floats and other swimming/training aids, tables, chairs, bleacher seating, cleaning equipment, etc.: minimum of 30 m^2 and up to 75 m^2 or more. Also, storage may be required for various equipment and seating for the main sports hall: from 50 m^2 (small hall) to 115 m^2 or more (large hall).

Storage for cleaning equipment (floor cleaning machines, buckets, mops, cleaning materials, etc.) and general equipment (spare light bulbs, access ladders, etc.) must be provided.

Stores should be kept fairly shallow (about 5.5 m deep maximum) and may require direct access from outside for deliveries. All doors and access routes will need to be a minimum of 2.25 m high and preferably 2.7 m. Where movable bleacher seating is used the minimum height must be 2.85 m.

Plant rooms

Detailed information regarding equipment and requirements should be obtained from appropriate consultants and specialist manufacturers/suppliers. Ventilation must be adequate and care must be taken to ensure safe disposal of fumes (chlorine gas, boiler fumes, etc.). Floor should be non-slip with rapid drainage. In large plant rooms overhead lifting gear and girder may be required.

These are necessary for water treatment and filtration, heating, ventilation, electrical substation, etc. Space requirements will depend on size of complex, size of pool – plant room for pool can be based on 50–60% of water area – systems used, and the requirements of the various authorities involved. Approximate area required for medium–large complex (total area ±4,000 m^2) would be in the region of 250–300 m^2. Separate store (about 10 m^2) will be required for chemical storage. Cold water storage – usually at high level – of about 80 m^2 will be required.

Spaces should be grouped together and sited so as to minimise the length of service runs. Certain spaces (electrical substation and chemical store) will require direct access from the outside. A service yard is desirable.

A workshop and storage for spare parts may be required.

2.26   Building design

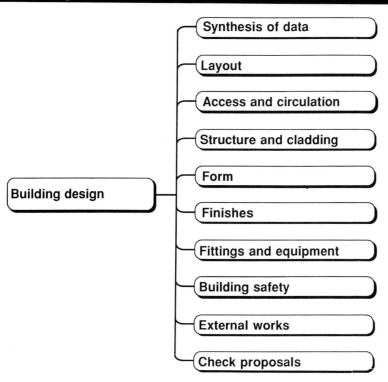

Synthesis of data

Bring together all requirements and constraints in terms of particular aspects of building design. Consider implications of all detailed data with regard to design policies and modify if required. Confirm or adjust space standards to be used for project.

Layout

Develop layout to meet site, circulation, constructional, environmental, statutory, economic and other requirements. Consider in particular the effects of:

— phasing.
— growth and change – a design based too rigidly on specific requirements may not be satisfactory for long.
— fixed spaces (lifts, stairs, lavatories, ducts, etc.) – locate in position favourable to future addition and flexibility.
— relationship to any existing or future adjacent building and/or outdoor facilities which may form part of complex.

With new information available it may be necessary to change an idea which was (or seemed) right at an earlier stage. See 2.25.1-4 for basic information on relationships between main spaces. See also 2.17.

Access and circulation

When deciding location and relationship of spaces, and patterns of circulation, consider:

See Appendix A.1.b: *New Metric Handbook*[11], chapter 6. Ramp design for the disabled should be based on the expected types of users: ambulant disabled or persons in wheelchairs, etc. Generally speaking, gradients for long ramps should not exceed 1:12 and for short-rise ramps 1:9. Doorways (and, if possible, both leaves of double doors – for example, at entrance) likely to be used by persons in wheelchairs should be at least 840 mm wide. See also Walter[13].

— access from outside for: users, staff, goods vehicles, other vehicles (ambulances).
— use of automatic door(s) at main entrance; also problem of door thresholds, doormats and door furniture.
— internal circulation of people: users of wet and dry facilities; users of special facilities such as squash courts and indoor bowling rink; the disabled; spectators; staff.
— colour coding for easy identification.
— access points to all viewing areas to be clearly identified.
— circulation within changing/shower areas for users of wet and dry facilities.
— links between changing-rooms and activity areas to be as direct as possible.
— management rules affecting circulation, for example, dress in refreshment areas.
— movement of large pieces of equipment, for example, from delivery to stores and stores to activity areas.
— movement between outdoor facilities (if any) and shared use of indoor facilities, for example, changing-rooms.
— vertical circulation: lifts, escalators, stairs, ramps.
— main and secondary control points.
— internal access to emergency exits required by fire regulations.

Structure and cladding

See Appendix A.1.b: *AJ Handbook of Building Structure*[28] and *AJ Handbook of Building Enclosure*[29]; also *Handbook of Sports and Recreational Building Design*[1], Vol. 1 p.112 and Vol. 2 p.114. For information on energy conservation by the design of building fabric see Gage[30] and Markus[31].

Develop and integrate structural proposals in the light of layout, for example, bay spacing and spans to meet layout planning requirements. When assessing structure and cladding consider:

— long spans over pool hall and main sports hall as well as the height of these spaces.
— condensation and protection from corrosion.
— thermal insulation: solar gain and heat loss, and movement.
— services integration: flexibility and accessibility can affect design of roof in particular.
— strength to carry a variety of equipment both fixed and movable.
— fire and safety: free-standing and projecting columns can be a hazard.

Form

See also 2.17.

Develop form of building in light of layout, structural and environmental aspects.

Finishes

See 2.25.1.

When selecting internal finishes consider:

— robustness, ease of cleaning, and minimum maintenance.
— colour and surface reflectance.
— safety: non-slip floors and non-abrasive walls up to 2 to 3 m from floors.

— effect on general environment which should be light and pleasant.
— noise, for example, sound-absorbent ceilings.

Fittings and equipment

Determine:

— position of fixing plates, tracks, sockets, etc. for swimming-pool, gymnastic and other equipment.
— the effect of building-in fixings on walls and floors: floor slabs may need to be thickened at these points.
— position, type and fixing of all fittings including signs.
— consider vandalism: components and their fixings must be robust and not invite interference.
— cost: initial and long term.

See Appendix A.1.b: *Handbook of Sports and Recreational Building Design*[1], Vol. 1 pp.119 and 128; Vol. 2 p.139; also Dawes[20], chapter 11.

Building safety

Investigate all requirements for safety and ensure that efforts are made to eliminate possible hazards. Consider:

— safe movement: stairwells and passages wide enough and free of obstructions (fixtures should be recessed); floors non-slip and properly drained in wet areas.
— provision of suitable hand- and/or guard-rails where necessary.
— toughened glass in all viewing areas.
— changing-rooms and swimming-pool on same level.
— adequate space between playing areas and walls/spectator seating.
— proper lighting in all activity and circulation areas.
— accessibility of rescue and life-support equipment.
— visual and sound-warning systems for the deaf/hard of hearing, and the visually impaired.
— braille markers or use of textured surfaces to relay information to the visually impaired.

External works

Develop landscape and siting proposals in light of building design proposals, statutory requirements, and other factors. Consider:

— access: roadways, pathways and links to outdoor facilities and/or adjacent or adjoining buildings.
— planting and other landscape features.
— parking areas; bicycle racks.
— outdoor lighting and external signs.

For car parking allow 20–$30\,m^2$ per space; for pedal and motor cycles $1.5\,m^2$ per space. For detail information see Appendix A.1.b: *New Metric Handbook*[11], Chapters 7 and 40.

Check proposals

Check that all objectives, resources, constraints, risks and implications of users, and other, requirements have been taken into consideration in the overall design. Consider all possible conflicts, trade-offs and balances:

— layout in terms of openness *versus* staffing as well as internal environment control.

— flexibility *versus* form and cost of structure and services; also in terms of variety of space and character.

— floor areas against original estimates.

2.27 Environmental control

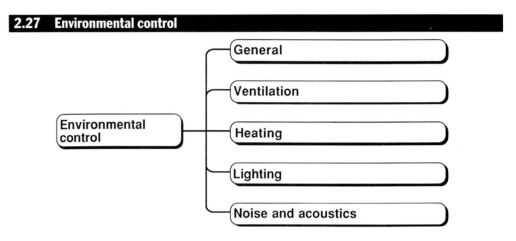

General

Close co-operation between all members of the design team is particularly important. See Appendix A.1.b: Gage[30] and Markus[31].

Develop and integrate environmental installation proposals to meet layout, constructional, statutory and economic requirements. Consider installation as whole – no one aspect in isolation.

Ventilation

Climate and the shape of the building will influence extent to which mechanical ventilation will be needed. Approximate requirements (air changes/hour): activity areas – 3–5; pool hall – 4–8; toilets – 5–8; showers and changing-rooms – 8–10. For more detailed information see Appendix A.1.b: *New Metric Handbook*[11], Chapter 41.

Determine best and most economical method of ensuring adequate and flexible ventilation for various spaces. Consider the basic alternatives:

— natural ventilation: can be satisfactory for most areas.

— full fresh air mechanical ventilation with no recirculation: pool halls and shower (pre-cleanse) areas because of high moisture content, chemicals and body odours.

— mechanical ventilation with recirculation: ozone will have to be used in swimming-pool water treatment system; dehumidification will also be necessary.

Consider position of air inlets and outlets/extract fans; air velocity and movement patterns are important, for example, they must not affect flight of shuttlecocks in sports hall.

Heating

Determine best and most economical method of heating various spaces:

—   radiant heating systems.

—   underfloor elements.

—   warm air: central system or local fan convectors.

Determine method of heating water:

—   low pressure hot water system served from central boiler(s).

—   storage cylinder (with immersion heater) for showers, etc.

—   individual instantaneous heaters for showers and wash-basins: particularly where these are only requirements for hot water.

—   non-storage calorifier for pool water.

—   solar-assisted heat pump.

As ventilation (for example, pool hall, shower area, etc.) accounts for large heat loss, consider heat-recovery system.

Climate, as well as shape and structure of building, will influence solar gain and heat loss and, therefore, heating requirements. Approximate temperatures to which spaces should be heated: activity areas – 12 to 16°C; changing and pre-cleanse – ±27°C; pool hall – 27 to 28°C; other areas – 20 to 21°C. Water temperatures required: main pool – 24 to 26°C; learner pool – 28 to 30°C. System may need to be flexible to permit rapid adjustment to suit the range of activities provided for. Storage capacity for hot water: around 0.22 m³/shower.

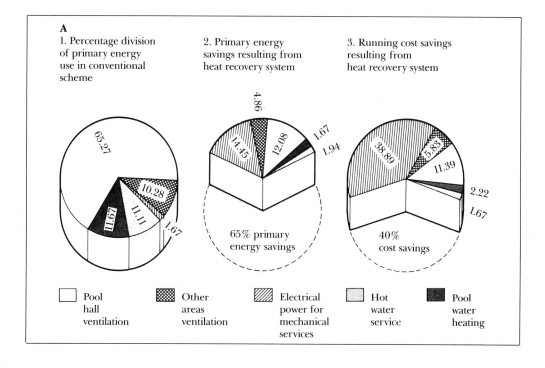

A

1. Percentage division of primary energy use in conventional scheme

2. Primary energy savings resulting from heat recovery system

3. Running cost savings resulting from heat recovery system

☐ Pool hall ventilation   ▨ Other areas ventilation   ▨ Electrical power for mechanical services   ☐ Hot water service   ■ Pool water heating

Fig. 2.21   *Energy saving at Bury St Edmunds rebuilt sports cente (see Figs. 3.10–3.16, p.141) where the opportunity was taken to completely reorganise the heating and ventilating system which was centralised to make heat recovery easy.*

A: the 'electrical' refers to mechanical services and does not include lighting. The left-hand diagram is an updated version of the original sports centre scheme, but the figures have been adjusted to be comparable with the central diagram, for example, the previous scheme had 0.5 air changes per hour whereas the new scheme has five air changes. The left-hand diagram assumes the five air changes. The previous scheme had heating in the squash courts; the new scheme does not.

B and C: Sankey diagrams showing the energy savings that can be achieved by adopting heat recovery at a sports centre quite similar to Bury St Edmunds. These diagrams are not indicative in detail of actual performance at the rebuilt Bury St Edmunds, although the principles illustrated in the heat recovery system (C) are similar. For further information on the project, see The Architects' Journal, *24 March 1982.*

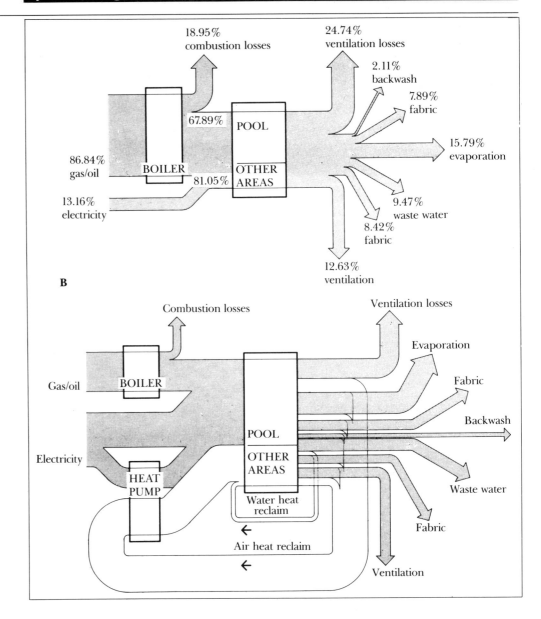

Lighting

Consider lighting requirements of various spaces:

— natural lighting: correct position and sizes of glazed areas to avoid glare, reflections, and unwanted solar gain and heat loss; also to provide uniform illumination.

— screening of glazed areas: blinds, planting, etc.

— safety glass for protection of low-level glazing.

— artificial lighting: quality of light, efficiency, length of life, initial and ongoing costs. Select type (fluorescent, high-pressure sodium and mercury or luminous ceiling) and position: ceiling-mounted (uplighters and/or

For details of approximate levels of lighting required see 2.25.1, 2 and 4. Particular care must be taken with lighting for certain activities (badminton and table tennis); specialist advice should be obtained. See also Appendix A.1.b: *Handbook of Sports and Recreational Building Design*[1], Vol. 1 p.125; Vol. 2 p.120; also *New Metric Handbook*[11], Chapter 43 and *CIBS Lighting Guide: Sports*[27].

downlighters) or wall/track-mounted floodlights.
— uniformity of illuminance: spaces must be free of areas of high and low levels of lighting.
— special lighting: vapour-proof fittings in certain areas; underwater lighting in pool; high illuminances required for TV.
— shielding of fittings and/or impact-resistant transparent covers.
— emergency lighting: generator or batteries; automatic changeover device; separate circuit to light strategic routes and exits.
— means of access to lighting and glazed areas (for example, rooflights) for maintenance and cleaning, repair and replacement.
— flexibility of lighting system (various switching possibilities) to suit multiple use of spaces.
— dimmer switches on certain fittings: lighting in spectator areas, etc.
— lighting control from central point: reception office.

Noise and acoustics

Ensure that the following factors have been considered:
— layout of building to minimise nuisance from noisy areas, for example, squash courts, and location of doors and windows.
— 45dB reduction between noisy areas and other spaces where noise would disturb.
— reverberation time in each space: absorption and reflection qualities of all surfaces.
— sound-absorbent materials impervious to moisture where necessary.
— installation of machinery likely to create problems (for example, through vibration or impact sounds) on floating or resilient mountings.

For general data on sound see Appendix A.1.b: *New Metric Handbook*[11], Chapter 44.

2.28   Services and security

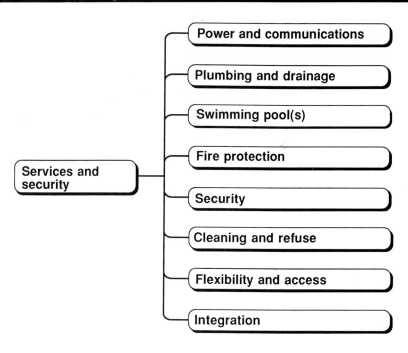

Power and communications

Consider:

See Appendix A.1.b: Corby[24] and *Communications*[25]; also *Handbook of Sports and Recreational Building Design*[1], Vol. 1 p.128 (automatic officiating equipment) and Vol. 2 p.153 (facilities for TV and radio broadcasting). Computer and other electronic technology is evolving so rapidly that specialist advice should be obtained at an early stage.

— realistic sizes for vertical and horizontal ducts; also extent and method of providing flexibility: outlets (power and communications) installed where needed on trunking.

— power points in all spaces for: sound-amplifiers and record-players; electronic and other special equipment (sauna stove, solarium lamps, plant room equipment); floor and pool cleaning machines, etc.

— cable installation and outlets for computer equipment, electronic judging apparatus and scoreboards, closed-circuit television, etc.

— special requirements for video recording and transmission; TV and radio broadcasts; automatic ticket and entrance control machines, etc.; also for all plant room equipment.

— outlet points for staff and public telephones; internal telephone system; loudspeaker (public address) and signalling systems.

Establish detailed requirements for sub-station and distribution/meter rooms; also switchboard. Consider:

— access for maintenance.

— sound insulation.

Plumbing and drainage

Determine requirements for hot and cold water, and drainage installations. Consider:

— position and size of ducts.
— position and space for water tank.
— water connections for vending machines; hose-points for floor washing, etc.
— water supply for fire sprinklers and/or hose-reels.
— requirements for boiler room (if needed); also access for maintenance.

Swimming-pool(s)

Decide on water treatment and circulation system for pool(s).

— investigate characteristics of local water supply.
— disinfecting agent to be used (chlorine, ozone, bromine).
— system for controlling pH of water – will depend on choice of disinfecting agent.
— water turnover times (generally once every three hours for main pool); affects design of treatment plant; pipes, pumps and filters.
— pattern of water circulation within pool: where water is to be introduced (shallow end, one long side, both sides, all around, etc.) and extracted (deep end, sides of surface channels, bottom, etc.).
— consider pool edge details; level deck, skimmer weirs, overflow channels, etc.

Consult specialists: also local health officer and water authority. Public swimming-pools must comply with DOE Public Health standards (revised 1976). In the USA various organisations including APHA (American Public Health Association Inc), NSPI and the Underwriters Laboratory have published suggested standards. For detailed information refer to Appendix A.1.b: *Handbook of Sports and Recreational Building Design*[1], Vol. 1 pp. 93–104; Dawes[20], Chapters 13 and 15; and Perkins[21], Chapter 7. Note: level (or top) deck pools – where water level is the same as pool surrounds – are widely adopted; there is little difference in cost between this method and the traditional overflow channel system.

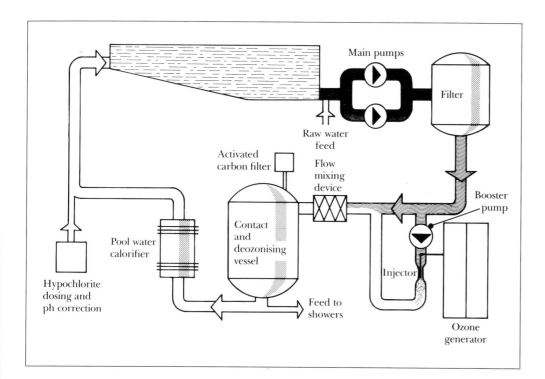

Fig. 2.22 *Pool water treatment system using ozone. Reductions in the use of energy for indoor swimming-pools can be achieved by the application of heat recovery to their heating and ventilating plant, for example by using a heat pump (see Fig. 2.23, p.114). Maximum reduction of energy costs can be achieved if ozone is used for disinfection, because the elimination of chlorinous odour allows 75–80 per cent of the heated air to be recirculated and dehumidified, with a consequent reduction in the heating requirements for fresh air. The use of ozone helps to create a more pleasant environment for both swimmer and spectator.*

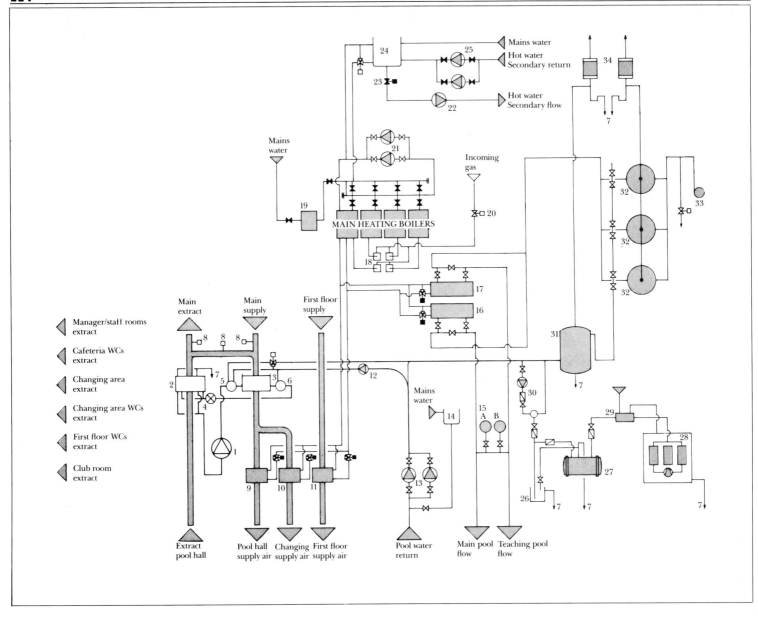

Fig. 2.23 *Diagrammatic layout of services at the Elswick Park Pool (see Figs. 3.5–3.9, p. 140). Ozone is used as a disinfectant allowing air extracted from the pool hall to be dehumidified – by means of a heat pump which also acts as a cooling coil in summer – and recirculated. Heat reclaimed from the dehumidification and cooling is used to reheat the pool water and incoming fresh air. The four gas-fired boilers provide low-temperature hot water for the heating system. (From* The Architects' Journal, *2 September 1981, p.457).*

1 Heat pump
2 Heat reclaim coil (evaporator)
3 Reclaimed heat input (condenser)
4 Expansion valve
5 Water heater
6 Sub cooler
7 Drain
8 Motorized damper
9 Re-heat battery pool hall
10 Re-heat battery changing area
11 Heater battery first floor

12 Pool water heat reclaim pump
13 Pool water circulating pumps
14 Pool water -make-up tank
15 dosing units
    A acid
    B sodium hypo
16 Main pool calorifier
17 Teaching pool calorifier
18 Gas boosters
19 Pressurisation unit
20 Solenoid valve
21 Heating pumps
22 Hot water booster pump

23 Hot water high limit
24 Hot water storage
25 Hot water pumps
26 Water seal
27 Ozone generator
28 Air dryer
29 Air cooler
30 Water mixing equipment
31 Reaction tank
32 Pool water filter
33 Air blower
34 Ozone wasting equipment

Fire protection

Establish requirements in terms of national legislation and local by-laws, for example:

— fire-resistance of walls and doors.

— means of escape for occupants.

Consider the following precautionary measures:

— smoke exhaust/extraction system.

— minimum use of combustible materials and equipment.

— detector system: sensors actuated by heat, rapid rise in heat, presence of smoke, etc.

— extinguishers: automatic sprinkler system; hose-reels; portable extinguishers.

— alarms: connected to automatic detector system and central indicator panel; also, possibly, direct link to local fire station.

Fire precautions should be discussed with the local fire authority and fire insurers. For general information see Appendix A.1.b: *Thinking About Fire*[22].

Security

Ascertain requirements for protection of building from possible break in. Consider:

— overall objectives: what system is required to do; what areas need special protection, etc.

— forms of detectors: perimeter (windows and doors); volumetric or acoustic devices, etc.

— type of alarm: audible or silent (signalling control centre of alarm company or police) or combination (micro-processor programmed to respond in various ways).

— special storage/protection for valuable items; provision for locking service windows, counters, etc.

— security lighting.

— problem of cleaners moving through the centre and/or other activities outside normal opening hours.

Specialist advice should be obtained at an early stage. For detailed information see Appendix A.1.b: *Security in Buildings*[23]

Cleaning and refuse

Establish how cleaning will be done and at what times; amount of refuse that accumulates weekly and method and frequency of disposal. Consider special provision for storage of cleaning materials and equipment, and refuse-bins.

Flexibility and access

Consider flexibility of services arrangement and ease of access for maintenance, inspection and modification.

Integration

Consider integration of the services plant and distribution spaces into the structure.

2.29 Completion of phase

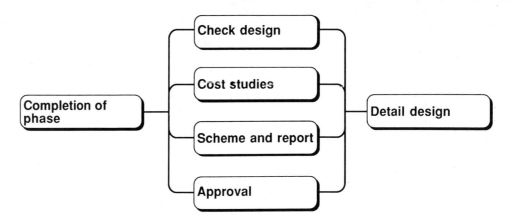

Check design

Check design proposal against recorded requirements:
— can all facilities required by client/users in fact be accommodated?
— confirm that all statutory requirements have been taken into account and verify that proposal meets with approval of all relevant bodies.

Cost studies

Make detailed cost estimates of building and services installation, site work, etc. Also estimates of running cost – particularly those affected by design proposals, for example, staffing, maintenance, heating and cooling.
Verify that proposed design can be built within budget: modify if required.

Scheme and report

Present comprehensive proposal to client in clear and concise format:
— drawings, models, sketches.
— independent reports from each consultant with reasons for recommendations and appropriate analytical evidence for the selection of particular proposals.
— cost analysis.

Approval

Obtain client's approval before proceeding to detail design.

2.30 Detail design

This guide is not continued beyond the phase outlined in 2.29: by that phase all major factors in the project should have been considered. This phase is concerned with completing the scheme in increasing depth of detail, something that is common to all projects.

Note: any changes to the basic design after this point will cause delay and cost money.

See Appendix A.1.a: 'Plan of Work', Stage E in *Architect's Job Book*; and Green.

APPENDICES

A.1 References and sources of information

a. References: Section 1

1 Jones, J. Christopher, *Design Methods: Seeds of Human Futures*, Chichester: Wiley, 1981.
2 Palmer, M. A., *The Architect's Guide to Facility Programming*, Washington: American Institute of Architects, 1981.
3 Preiser, W.(ed.), *Facility Programming: methods and applications*, Stroudsburg, Pa.: Dowden, Hutchinson & Ross, 1978.
4 Sanoff, H., *Methods of Architectural Programming*, Stroudsburg, Pa.: Dowden, Hutchinson & Ross, 1977.
5 Alexander, C. *et al., A Pattern Language: Towns, Buildings, Construction*, New York: Oxford University Press, 1977.
6a Elder, A. J., *Guide to the Building Regulations 1976* (7th edition), London: The Architectural Press, 1981. To be read in conjunction with:
6b Elder, A. J., *Guide to the Second Amendment 1981*, London: The Architectural Press, 1982.
7 Speaight, A. & Stone, G., *The AJ Legal Handbook* (3rd edition), London: The Architectural Press, 1982.
8 Mazria, E., *The Passive Solar Energy Book* (Expanded professional edition), Emmaus, Pa: Rodale Press, 1979.
9 Koenigsberger, O. H. *et al., Manual of Tropical Housing and Building*, Part 1: Climatic Design, London: Longman, 1973.

Other useful general references:

An Introduction to Cost Planning, London: The Royal Institution of Chartered Surveyors, 1976.
Architect's Job Book, compiled by L. Beaven and D. Dry (4th edition), London: RIBA Publications, 1983.
Bathurst, P. E. & Butler, D. A., *Building Cost Control Techniques* (2nd edition),

London: Heinemann, 1980.

Cartlidge, D. P. & Mehrtens, I. N., *Practical Cost Planning*, London: Hutchinson, 1982.

Cross, N. & Roy, R., *Design Methods Manual* (*Man-made Futures:* Units 13-16), Milton Keynes: The Open University, 1975.

Ferry, D. J., *Cost Planning of Buildings* (4th edition revised by T. Brandon), London: Granada, 1980.

Green, R. *The Architect's Guide to Running a Job* (Amended edition), London: The Architectural Press, 1980.

Kemper, A. M., *Architectural Handbook: environmental analysis, architectural programming, design and technology, and construction*, New York: Wiley, 1979.

Lacy, R. E., *Climate and Building in Britain*, London: HMSO, 1978.

Longmore, J., *BRS Daylight Protractors*, London: HMSO, 1968.

Lynch, K., *Site Planning* (2nd edition), Cambridge, Mass.: MIT Press, 1971.

Powell, J. (ed.), *Handbook of Architectural Practice and Management* (4th edition), London: RIBA Publications, 1980.

Seeley, I. H., *Building Economics: appraisal and control of building costs and efficiency* (2nd edition), London: Macmillan, 1976.

Stone, P. A., *Building Design Evaluation: costs in use* (3rd edition), London: Spon, 1980.

b.   References: Section 2

1   Geraint, J. and Heard, H. (eds), *Handbook of Sports and Recreational Building Design* (Vol. 1: 'Ice Rinks and Swimming-Pools'; Vol. 2: 'Indoor Sports'; Vol. 3: 'Outdoor Sports'; Vol. 4: 'Sports Data'), London: The Architectural Press, 1981.

2   'Update: Indoor Sports and Recreation', *The Architects' Journal*, Vol. 177, 23 March, 30 March, 6 April and 13 April 1983.

3   *A Question of Balance*, 2 vols, Edinburgh: Scottish Sports Council, 1979.

4   Coopers & Lybrand Associates, *Sharing Does Work: The Economic and Social Costs and Benefits of Joint and Direct Sports Provision*, London: Sports Council, 1980.

5   Duffield, B. S., Best, J. P. & Collins, M. F., *A Digest of Sports Statistics*, London: Sports Council, 1983.

6   *Sport in the Community: the next 10 years*, London: Sports Council, 1982.

7   Perrin, G. A., *Design for Sport*, Sevenoaks: Butterworth, 1981.

8   Burchell, R. & Listokin, D., *The Adaptive Re-use Handbook: procedures to inventory, control, manage and re-employ surplus municipal properties*, New Jersey: Rutgers University Press, 1981.

9   Cantacuzino, S. & Brandt, S., *Saving Old Buildings*, London: The Architectural Press, 1980.

10   *Sport for All in Converted Buildings*, Vol. 2, London: Sports Council, 1978.

11   Tutt, P. & Adler, D. (eds), *New Metric Handbook*, London: The Architectural Press, 1979.

12   Perrin, G. A., *Sports Halls & Swimming-Pools: a design and briefing guide*, London: Spon, 1980.

13 Walter, F., *Sports Centres and Swimming-Pools* (2nd edition), Edinburgh: Thistle Foundation, 1974.

14 Goldsmith, S., *Designing for the Disabled* (3rd edition), London: RIBA Publications, 1976.

15 Harkness, S. & Groom, J. N., *Building Without Barriers for the Disabled*, New York: Whitney, 1976.

16 *Office Space: a primer for users and designers*, London: HMSO, 1976.

17 Duffy, F., Cave, C. & Worthington, J., *Planning Office Space*, London: The Architectural Press, 1978.

18 Lawson, F., *Principles of Catering Design* (2nd edition), London: The Architectural Press, 1978.

19 Davis, B., *The Traditional English Pub: a way of drinking*, London: The Architectural Press, 1981.

20 Dawes, J., *Design and Planning of Swimming-Pools*, London: The Architectural Press, 1979.

21 Perkins, P. H., *Swimming-Pools* (2nd edition), London: Applied Science Publishers, 1978.

22 'Thinking About Fire', *The Architects' Journal*, Vol. 176, 11 August, 18 August and 8 September 1982.

23 'Security in Buildings', *The Architects' Journal*, Vol. 171, 28 May 1980 *et seq.*

24 Corby, M., Donohue, E. J. & Hamer, M., *Telecomms Users' Handbook*, London: Telecommunications Press, 1982.

25 'Communications', *The Architects' Journal*, Vol. 176, 4 August 1982.

26 *Swimming-Pools: requirements for competition*, Loughborough: Amateur Swimming Association, 1977.

27 *CIBS Lighting Guide: Sports*, London: Chartered Institute of Building Services, 1974.

28 Hodgkinson, A., *AJ Handbook of Building Structure* (2nd edition), London: The Architectural Press, 1980.

29 Vandenberg, M. & Elder, A. J. (eds), *AJ Handbook of Building Enclosure*, London: The Architectural Press, 1974.

30 Gage, M. & Murphy, I., *Design and Detailing for Energy Conservation*, London: The Architectural Press, 1983.

31 Markus, T. A. & Morris, E. N., *Buildings, Climate and Energy*, London: Pitman, 1980.

Other useful references:

(See also Bibliography *The Architects' Journal*, 13 April 1983, p.89):

* Diamant, R. M. E., *Energy Conservation Equipment*, London: The Architectural Press, 1984.

* *Planning Facilities for Athletics, Physical Education and Recreation* (revised edition), North Palm Beach, Fla: The Athletic Institute & American Alliance for Health, Physical Education, Recreation, and Dance, 1979.

* *Saving Energy in Swimming-Pools and Leisure Centres*, London: British Gas Corporation, 1981.

* Templeton, D. & Lord, P., *Detailing for Acoustics*, London: The Architectural Press, 1983.

* Thompson, N., *Sports Facilities for Disabled People*, London: The Architectural Press, 1983.

* Tipp, G. & Watson, V. J., *Polymeric Surfaces for Sports and Recreation*, London: Applied Science Publishers, 1982.

c. Sources of information (general): UK

Ordnance Survey
Romsey Road
Maybush
Southampton SO9 4DH
Tel. 0703-775555

The central survey and mapping organisation in the public sector. Produces and maintains up-to-date basic surveys at 1:1,250 for major urban areas, and at 1:2,500 (minor towns and cultivated areas) or 1:10,000 (mountain and moorland) for the remainder of the country; also a range of special maps and services. Catalogues and various leaflets are available from address given; maps obtainable through booksellers and OS agents.

The need to reproduce OS publications in whole or part is provided for by a scale of royalty charges and a series of licences designed to meet the needs of various authorities, organisations and the professions. Full information is given in OS leaflets No. 8 and No. 23.

Institute of Geological Sciences
Geological Museum
Exhibition Road
South Kensington
London SW7 2DE
Tel. 01-589 3444
also:
Murchison House
West Mains Road
Edinburgh EH9 3LA
Tel. 031-667 1000

Geological survey maps are available at a scale of 1:63,360 (1 in.) (when reprinted these sheets are generally being replaced by sheets at 1:50,000, new sheets are published at 1:50,000 only) with special areas available at 1:25,000 and 1:10,560 (6 in.). Memoirs describing the geology, including details of sections, bore holes and other data have been published for many of the sheets. A catalogue of maps is available from the Institute who provide advisory services on a wide range of economic and environmental topics.

The museum contains a collection of building stones from most quarries now working stone in the UK, as well as marbles and other ornamental stones from most countries of the world. The library contains material covering the geological sciences literature of the world and is open to members of the public for reference purposes.

Meteorological Office
London Road
Bracknell
Berkshire RG12 2SZ
Tel. 0344-20242
also:
231 Corstorphine Road
Edinburgh EH12 7BB
Tel. 031-334 9721
and:
Tyrone House
Ormeau Avenue
Belfast BT2 8HH
Tel. 0232-28457
Weather information for sites in the UK (and abroad) to help with analysis and design; also provides a range of services including CLIMEST, a quick-reply service to assist the construction industry.
Various publications available (listed in leaflet No. 12). Library is open to the public and contains material covering, amongst other things, all aspects of meteorology and climatology and a large collection of world-wide data.

Department of the Environment
Air Photographs Unit
6th Floor
Prince Consort House
Albert Embankment
London SE1 7TP
A large range of aerial photography – photographs, negatives and microfilm – and a Central Register of Air Photography which contains, amongst other things, information on the coverage and scale of commercial photography.
Copies of material are available for sale.

Department of the Environment
Map Library
5th Floor
Prince Consort House
Albert Embankment
London SE1 7TP
The map library holds an extensive collection covering many aspects of town and country planning and local government mostly of England and Wales. Selected maps are for sale – details and prices available on application.

Aerofilms Ltd
Gate Studios
Station Road
Boreham Wood
Herts WD6 1EJ
Tel. 01-207 0666
Oblique aerial photography to order from a library collection (covering a variety of subjects including meteorology, geology, building construction, architecture) in black-and-white, and colour. Free proofs submitted on request; print prices and reproduction fees supplied on request. Stereo pairs available as paper prints, 35 mm slides and overhead projector transparencies.

Office of Population Censuses and Surveys
St. Catherine's House
10 Kingsway
London WC2B 6JP
Tel. 01-242 0262
Library contains population census and vital statistics reports from most countries. Open to general public (preferably by appointment).

Building Research Establishment
1) Building Research Station
Bucknalls Lane
Garston
Watford
Herts WD2 7JR
Tel. 09273-74040
2) Fire Research Station
Borehamwood
Herts WD6 2BL
Tel. 01-953 6177
3) Princes Risborough Laboratory
Princes Risborough
Aylesbury
Bucks
Tel. 084-44 3101

also:
BRE (Scottish Laboratory)
Kelvin Road
East Kilbride
Strathclyde G75 OR2
Tel. 03552-33941

The BRS covers building design and construction, environmental design, etc.; the Fire Research Station is concerned with fire extinction and prevention, structural aspects of fire in buildings, means of escape, etc.; the Princes Risborough Laboratory deals with the use of timber, wood-based and other materials in building.

Details of advisory services and publications are available from each station.

British Services Research and Information Association
Old Bracknell Lane West
Bracknell
Berks
Tel. 0344-25071
A non-profit-making association. The provision of information and advice is one of its main functions. Membership includes consulting engineers, contractors, manufacturers and others concerned with mechanical and electrical services of buildings.

British Standards Institution
2 Park Street
London W1A 2BS
Tel. 01-629 9000
Recognised body for the preparation and promulgation of standards including performance and constructional specifications and codes of practices. Enquiry service and publications available. The library contains complete sets of British Standards as well as foreign and international standards. It is open to the general public.

Fire Protection Association
Aldermary House
Queen Street
London EC4N 1TJ
Tel. 01-248 5222
Central advisory organisation (set up by insurers) covering all aspects of fire prevention and control. Provides an information service and will give technical and general advice on fire protection both at design stage and in the maintenance of buildings. Library facilities may be used by the public (preferably by appointment). A list of publications is available.

HM Stationery Office
Atlantic House
Holborn Viaduct
London EC1P 1BN
Tel. 01-583 9876
Produces hundreds of publications each year for Parliament, Government departments, museums and other public institutions in the UK.

The most useful guides are the sectional lists. These, and all HMSO publications, can be obtained from HMSO bookshops (London, Edinburgh, Manchester, Birmingham, Cardiff, Bristol and Belfast) or from booksellers appointed as stockists.

National Association of Building Centres
26 Store Street
London WC1E 7ET
Tel. 01-637 1022
Represents all building centres in the UK and Ireland with the object of co-ordinating their functions and services. The individual centres usually have a permanent exhibition of building products and provide an enquiry/advisory service. Information on the individual centres may be obtained from the National Association.

Central Council for the Disabled (Access for the Disabled)
34 Eccleston Square
London SW1
Tel. 01-821 1871
Provides a full advisory service on the design of buildings for the disabled. A list of publications on the subject is available.

Centre on Environment for the Handicapped
126 Albert Street
London NW1 7NF
Tel. 01-267 6111
Provides an advisory and information service on the design of buildings for the handicapped and for elderly people.

d. Sources of information (general): USA

US Geological Survey (Department of the Interior)
Topographic maps and indexes: benchmark locations, level data, and tables of elevations; streamflow data; water resources; geologic maps; horizontal control data; monument location.
Topographic maps available in 7½-minute (latitude and longitude) quadrangle size plotted to a scale of 1:62,500.
Geologic map of the US to a scale of 1:2,500,000.
Geologic quadrangle maps in various scales.
Mineral resource maps are also available.
An index map identifying published maps and publication date is available free from:
Map Information Service
US Geological Survey
12201 Sunrise Valley Drive
Reston, VA 22092

State Geological Surveys or equivalent state agencies
Geologic maps of most states to a scale of 1:500,000.
Mineral resource maps.

Army Map Service (Department of the Army)
Topographic maps in 7½-minute quadrangle size plotted to scale of 1:25,000; in 15-minute quadrangle size plotted to a scale of 1:50,000; and in 30-minute quadrangle size plotted to a scale of 1:125,000. Maps covering larger areas are prepared on scales of 1:250,000 and 1:500,000.

US National Ocean Survey (Department of Commerce)
Topographic maps; coastline charts; topographic and hydrographic studies of inland lakes and reservoirs; benchmark locations, level data, and tables of elevations; horizontal control data; seismological studies.

Soil Conservation Service (Department of Agriculture)
Local Soil Conservation Service Offices
or
Information Division
Soil Conservation Service
Washington DC 20250
Soil surveys generally covering one county (may cover several small counties or only parts of a large one) are published for all counties except Illinois. In this state the University of Illinois Agricultural Experimental Station publishes them. Surveys usually consist of maps that show the distribution of soils in the area, description of the soils, some suggestions as to their use and management, and general information about the area. An index is available.

Bureau of the Census
Census maps containing summarised population data are available for many different types and sizes of areas, for example, county, urbanised area, metropolitan and place maps. These are all available from either the Government Printing Office or the Central Users' Service.

Sanborn Map Company Inc.
Pelham NY
Sanborn fire insurance maps: these detailed maps of street layouts, building locations etc are used by insurance companies, governmental agencies, utility companies, banks, etc. Local fire insurance agents are equipped with Sanborn maps of their respective cities and towns; principal offices maintain complete nationwide files.

Bureau of Land Management
Township plots, showing land divisions, state maps, showing public land and reservations; survey progress map of the US, showing the progress of public-land surveys.

Mississippi River Commission (Department of the Army)
Hydraulic studies and flood control information.

US Forestry Service (Department of Agriculture)
Forest reserve maps including topography and culture and vegetation classification.

US Postal Service
Rural free delivery maps by counties, showing roads, streams, etc.

Local municipalities: county, city, town, village
Street maps, zoning maps, drainage maps, horizontal and vertical control data, utility maps.

US Department of Commerce: National Technical Information Service
Provides information on Government-sponsored research in different fields. Good reference material on earthquakes from annual bulletin: 'United States Earthquakes'.

US Weather Bureau and local weather stations
Historic data on weather conditions and maps of US climatic conditions.

Superintendent of Documents
Government Printing Office
Washington DC 20402
Daily weather maps published by the National Oceanic and Atmospheric Administrations Environmental Data Service. Also soil surveys, census maps, etc.

Agricultural Stabilisation Conservation Service (US Department of Agriculture):
Aerial Photography Division
Eastern laboratory
45 French Broad Avenue
Asheville
North Carolina 28802
also:
Western laboratory
2505 Parley's Way
Salt Lake City
Utah 84109

Aerial photographs of virtually any place in the US can be obtained from one of a number of sources. The ASCS has the greatest coverage of aerial photographs for the US of a single agency. To locate the agency holding a picture of a required area an index can be obtained from the Map Information Service of the US Geological Survey (see address above).

'Photogrammetric Engineering'
Magazine of the American Society of Photogrammetry
An informative guide to the organisations which can provide photogrammetric aerial maps.

e. Sources of information: sports

The Sports Council
16 Upper Woburn Place
London WC1H 0QP
Tel. 01-388 1277
also:
Sports Council for Wales
National Sports Centre for Wales
Sophia Gardens
Cardiff CF1 9SW
Tel. 0222-397571
and:
Scottish Sports Council
1 St Colme Street
Edinburgh EN3 6AA
Tel. 031-225 841
and:
Sports Council for Northern Ireland
2a Upper Malone Road
Belfast BT9 5LA
An independent body, The Sports Council was established by Royal Charter a decade ago to encourage wider participation in sport and physical recreation in Britain, and to increase the provision of facilities. There are separate Councils for Scotland, Wales and Northern Ireland, and a number of regional councils throughout England. The various councils operate schemes of financial assistance to increase the provision of new facilities and to stimulate fuller use of those already existing. Each council has its own criteria and policies for grant aid. Information and guidance should be sought at an early stage of any proposed project.
The Sports Council's Technical Unit for Sport consists of a team of building professionals who design sports facilities and are responsible for establishing good practice and providing guidance for designers and their clients.
A wide range of publications, from technical data and informed research on the latest developments in the world of sport and its provision, to reference material

and bibliographies are produced. A list is available on request; also available is a list of experienced consultants.

Department of the Environment
2 Marsham Street
London SW1P 3EB
Tel. 01-212 3434
This government department is responsible for the range of functions affecting the physical environment. These include recreation. Various publications dealing with, among other things, the purification of swimming-pool water, are produced and are available from HMSO bookshops.

Arts Council of Great Britain
105 Piccadilly
London W1V 0AU
Tel. 01-629 9495
Concerned with improving facilities for the arts, the Council – with Regional Arts Associations – will consider applications for grants towards the costs of the improvement or construction of centres when a recognisable and significant provision for professional or community arts activities is included.

National Playing Fields Association
25 Ovington Square
London SW3 1LQ
Tel. 01-584 6445
Sponsors research into recreational facilities and provide an information and advisory service. Will consider giving a modest low interest loan towards the cost of providing recreational facilities. Enquiries should be made at an early stage of a proposed project through the relevant County Playing Fields Association.

Institute of Baths and Recreation Management
Giffard House
36/38 Sherrard Street
Melton Mowbray
Leics LE13 1XJ
Tel. 0664-65531
A professional organisation for holders of the Institute's qualification. Associate membership is available to chartered architects, senior managers and engineers, and other approved persons engaged in the design, construction and management of swimming-pools and plant.
One of the main aims of the Institute is to promote improvements in the design, construction, equipment and maintenance of sports and recreation establishments, and it operates a National Advisory Service.
Publications on technical and specialist matters concerning the design and

operation of swimming-pools are produced; also an official journal 'Baths Service and Recreation Management'.

Institute of Leisure and Amenity Management
ILAM House
Lower Basildon
Reading RG8 9NE
Tel. 0491-873 558
Formed in January 1983 as the result of the amalgamation of a number of institutes/associations of recreation/entertainment managers. Every facet of management in the leisure profession is represented in the membership.
One of the principal objectives of the Institute is to further the knowledge of practising managers within the leisure and amenity profession, and to encourage the study of technical and related matters concerned with the planning, design, management and improvement of facilities, both private and commercial, for the benefit of the community at large.
The Institute provides a technical advice service. A list of publications is available on request.

Swimming-Pool and Allied Trades Association
Faraday House
17 Essendene Road
Caterham
Surrey CR3 5PB
Tel. Caterham 40110
To promote the sale of swimming-pools and related equipment and accessories, and to maintain standards of construction. An advisory service is available.

Note:
Current addresses of governing sports bodies in the UK can be obtained from The Sports Council.
In the USA contact:
American Alliance for Health, Physical Education, Recreation and Dance (AAHPERD)
1201 Sixteenth Street, NW
Washington DC 20036
Other organisations in the USA able to provide general information include:
The Athletic Institute
200 Castlewood Road
North Palm Beach
Florida 33408

American Public Health Association Inc.
1015 Eighteenth Street, NW
Washington DC 20036

National Swimming-Pool Institute
200 K Street, NW
Washington DC 20006

A.2 Site survey/ analysis

A. Geology and soil

Materials, processes, sources:
Soil survey maps and reports; geologic maps; aerial photographs. See Appendix A.1.c:
ERTS (Earth Resources Technology Satellite) images.
Trial holes (either dug pits or boreholes) with visual and tactile identification and/or laboratory testing of soil samples.
Building surveyor of local authority (UK).
Report from a geologist.

Data required:
(a) Underlying geology, rock character and depth.
(b) Soil type and depth: determine value as an engineering material (for example, safe bearing capacity) and as plant medium; also suitability for septic tanks, excavation, corrosion and frost heave potential; shrink/swell characteristics.
(c) Check drainage characteristics and for signs of fill, slides and subsidence.
(d) Possible use as a building material: adobe, brick, stone.

Limitations/danger signals:
— Swelling clay or peat.
— High salt content in soil.
— Signs of past landslides.
— Evidence of creep (slippage).
— Known earthquake faults.
— Volcanic areas.
— Underlayers of impermeable materials.
— Signs of erosion.
— Rock lying close to surface.
— Made up ground (filling) or undermining.

B. Topography

Materials, processes, sources:
ERTS images.
Topographical maps (useful for preliminary reconnaissance).
See Appendix A.1.c.
Geologic maps.
Aerial photographs: preferably in stereo pairs so

Data required:
(a) Height above sea level and geographical north point.
(b) Pattern of land forms.
(c) Contours, bench marks.
(d) Slope analysis, for example, orientation.

(e) Visibility analysis.
(f) Circulation analysis.
(g) Unique features.

that site can be viewed three-dimensionally.
Site survey by architect or land surveyor.
Computer-drawn illustrations can be useful to communicate the visual feeling of a land area.

Limitations/danger signals:
— Steep slopes (over 15 per cent).
— Undesirable slopes: west orientation, or slopes which block sun. Small buildable area. Possible problem of affecting sun-rights on adjacent properties.

C.   Hydrology

Data required:
(a) Existing water bodies: fluctuation and purity; flood levels.
(b) Natural and man-made drainage channels: flow, capacity, purity.
(c) Surface drainage pattern: amount, blockage, undrained depressions.
(d) Water table: elevation and fluctuation, springs.
(e) Underground water supply: quantity and quality.
(f) Potential for catching and storing surface water run-off in surface holding basin or underground tanks. Watersheds.

Materials, processes, sources:
Geologic maps.
Aerial photographs (infra-red is best for distinguishing between land and water).
ERTS images.
Local hydrological studies.
Trial holes (either dug pits at least 2 m deep or boreholes) dug during wet season.
Local health department for testing of water samples.
Visual inspection of existing structures.

Limitations/danger signals:
— High water table.
— Underground stream.
— Undrained areas: waterlogging.
— Site or portion of site located in flood plain (below known flood level).
— Streams or water bodies polluted by sewage or industrial waste.

D.   Vegetation/ecology

Data required:
(a) Dominant plant/animal communities: location and relative stability.
(b) Their dependence on existing factors, self-regulation and sensitivity to change.
(c) Mapping of general plant cover, including wooded areas.
(d) Specimen trees to be retained: their location, species, height and spread, and diameter at base.

Materials, processes, sources:
Report from a landscape architect; ecological survey.
Aerial photographs (infra-red is valuable for distinguishing between different types of vegetation and identifying areas of plant disease).
Geologic and topographic maps.
ERTS images.

Limitations/danger signals:
— Unique landscapes or those with fragile quality.
— Rare or unique flora or fauna.
— Habitat for wildlife or breeding ground.
— Migratory rest stops.
— Presence of insects (for example, mosquitoes, termites) or rodent breeding places.
— Poisonous reptiles and plants.

E. Climate

Materials, processes, sources:
Published weather data for region.
Data obtained from nearest weather station.
Solar charts, for example, cylindrical sun chart.
See Appendix A.1.a: Mazria[8]; Koenigsberger[9].
Solar radiation calculator and sliding calculator.
See Appendix A.1.a: Mazria[8].

Data required:

(a) Regional data on:

— monthly mean maximum and minimum temperatures.

— monthly mean maximum and minimum relative humidities.

— total average precipitation for each month; maximum rainfall for any 24-hour period; likelihood of driving rain and intensity.

— direction and force of prevailing winds; seasonal changes.

— sky conditions; cloudiness.

— average daily amounts of solar radiation for each month; sun angles – path of daily and seasonal sun.

— average annual and monthly snowfalls.

(b) Local microclimates: warm and cool slopes, air drainage, wind deflection and local breezes, shade, heat reflection and storage, plant indications.

(c) Noise levels, smell, atmospheric quality.

(d) Regional hazards: hail, tornadoes, lightning, sand and dust storms.

Limitations/danger signals:

— Lack of vegetation.

— Severe conditions (extreme heat or cold, strong winds, severe frost).

— Site situated in natural hazard belt.

— Odours, smoke and dust from industrial or other sources.

— Noise and vibration from traffic or trains; industrial or recreational sources, etc.

— Cold pockets in low-lying areas.

— Excessively windy, for example, crest or top of hill.

— Cold winter winds and wind tunnels.

F. Natural amenities

Data required:

(a) Character of visual spaces.

(b) Viewpoints, vistas.

(c) Quality and variation of light, sound, smell, feel.

Limitations/danger signals:

— Undesirable views or unpleasant character of one kind or another: barren, bleak, depressing, dirty, unfriendly, etc.

— Organisation providing for building funding, for example, building society.

— Insurance company.

— Licensing authorities.

— Fire brigade.

Man-made and cultural factors

A. Site values, rights and restraints

Data required:

(a) Determine municipal valuation, market price.

(b) Obtain existing drawings if available; dimensions, shape and area of site; exact position of boundaries.

(c) Status of property: form of ownership, easements, restrictions, rights of way, rights of access, zoning, density, floor space index, building lines, height restrictions, parking requirements, consents already received.

(d) History of site: rights of public and adjoining owners; public and private intentions for future use of site; possible conflicts; boundaries and party walls and fences. Ownership and condition; preservation orders on existing buildings or trees.

(e) Ascertain what consents are required and from which authorities they must be obtained; demolition requirements.

Materials, processes, sources:
Local authorities/agencies (county and/or city): building department, engineering department, transport and roads department, health department, town-planning department.
Private or public utilities, for example, post office.
Deeds office (county assessors – USA).
Factory inspectors.
Local authority building by-laws/regulations.

Limitations/danger signals:

— Adjacent sites that enjoy any easements against the site in question, for example, relating to drains and sewers or possibly a right to draw water from a well on the site.

— Possibility that planning permission for the project in question may not be given by the local authority or any other body from which consent must be obtained.

— Size or shape of site not suitable for type of proposed development and/or possible future expansion.

B. The surrounding area

Data required:

(a) Existing land uses and functions; possible future changes; historic trails and passageways; historic buildings; conservation areas.

(b) Relationship to surroundings; adequacy of local facilities: transport, schools, shops, postal service, housing, etc. What is within walking distance?

(c) Relationship to users, labour force, markets, existing sources of supply and services.

(d) Quality/character of neighbourhood and suitability for proposed project; effect of project on neighbourhood.

(e) Existing street layout and possible future changes; accessibility for all purposes; parking facilities.

(f) Possibility of extending site in future if necessary, for example, possibility of purchasing adjoining land.

Materials, processes, sources:
City and county land use and street maps.
City future development plans.

Limitations/danger signals:
— Future motorway or highway schemes that might affect project.
— Undesirable features in vicinity: tanneries, airports, railway sidings, highways or roads carrying heavy traffic, refuse dumps, radio activity, high tension wires, etc.
— Lack of public transport.
— Lack of diversity.
— Lack of schools, police, libraries, amusement, employment.
— Socially unattractive area.

Materials, processes, sources:
Visual observation; site and area survey.

C. Adjacent properties and existing buildings

Data required:
(a) Outline, location, elevations, type, condition and use of buildings on adjacent properties.
(b) Possible fire hazards; possible restraints, for example, unwanted shadows.
(c) Plans, elevations and construction details of existing buildings.
(d) Investigate condition and structural defects: signs of dry rot, beetles, damp patches, settlement cracks, loose plaster; condition of services and possibility of extension.

Limitations/danger signals:
— Buildings and trees on adjacent properties casting unwanted shadows particularly during colder months when sun is low.
— Existing buildings in vicinity showing signs of structural cracking.
— Undesirable views.
— Adjacent vacant or underused land which is vulnerable to change.

Materials, processes, sources:
Local authorities: engineers and surveyors, etc.
Water, electricity and gas boards or other appropriate authorities.
Post Office.

D. Services

Data required:
(a) Position, size and depth of public sewers and stormwater drains.
(b) Utility services available, for example, gas, water, electricity and telephone; positions, sizes, pressures, type of connections and type of supply (overhead or underground).
(c) Authority responsible for utility services; special requirements; costs for service and installation.
(d) Availability of and access to special services: garbage and rubbish removal, fire protection and other emergency services, street maintenance (for example, snow removal), etc.
(e) Potential for use of natural energy sources, for example, solar, wind and water.

Limitations/danger signals:
— High rates for services.
— Low water pressure.

A.3 Photographic illustrations

The following series of photographs will help to illustrate some of the many aspects that have been considered in sport and recreation design. Two things must be remembered, however: first, that in the space available it is possible to include only a few examples of different solutions, and that those shown are not necessarily the best alternatives in each case; secondly, that words and photographs are not architecture – the quality of the spaces, the lighting and acoustics, the equipment and finishes, and their effectiveness for the users can only be experienced, fairly examined and evaluated within the reality of the building itself.

Three contrasting sports and recreation centres are illustrated: a small local centre which is a conversion; an indoor swimming-pool situated in a public park; and a large sports centre, interesting because of lessons learned and incorporated after a fire.

The Jacksons Lane Community Centre in North London (Figs 3.1–3.4) is a converted Methodist church and hall which includes space for active recreation, refreshment and a theatre workshop on the ground floor, and for sports on the first floor which was built into the church nave. For a fuller description of this building see *The Architects' Journal* (30 March 1983, p.50).

Elswick Park Pool in Newcastle-upon-Tyne (Figs 3.5–3.9) is an expensive and elegant pavilion, glazed with smoked glass, situated in a remodelled park in a rather down-at-heel inner city area. The pool is half-way between being a competition pool – 25 m long with four lanes – and a fully fledged leisure pool; the cafeteria is designed to serve both the pool and the park. For a detailed study of this building see *The Architects' Journal* (2 September 1981).

Bury St Edmunds Sports Centre (Figs 3.10–3.16) was burned down in March 1980 during a gale and rebuilt in the following 18 months. Although the building's form, plan and structure closely follow that of its successful predecessor, it also incorporates improvements to correct shortcomings in the old building – including improved alarm and security systems – and to embody technical advances, particularly those of energy conservation. For a comprehensive study of this project see *The Architects' Journal* (24 March 1982).

3.1

Fig. 3.1   *The Methodist Church and hall which has been converted to a community centre, seen from Jacksons Lane.*

Fig. 3.2   *Jacksons Lane Community Centre before alterations.*

Fig. 3.3   *Ground and first-floor plans. A lift will eventually be installed to provide access to the sports floor for non-ambulant users.*

Fig. 3.4   *The new sports floor. When funds are available rebound boards will be installed up to dado level (photographer: Chris Schwarz).*

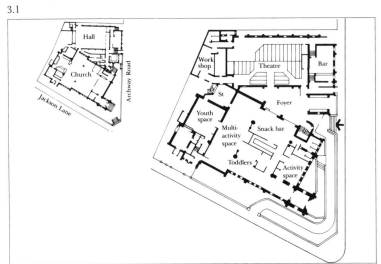

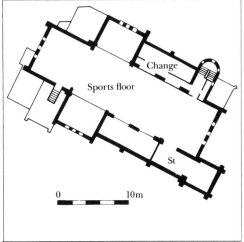

3.3

3.4

Fig. 3.5   *The south side of the Elswick Park pool (see plan) – the building acts as the architectural focus for the park. The steel lattice roof structure has a deep cantilever on this side (see Section b–b) to reduce glare in the pool area (photograph: City Engineer, Newcastle-upon-Tyne).*

Fig. 3.6   *Plans and sections.*

Fig. 3.7   *The shallow 'beach' of the learner pool is on the far left; the rectangular area with racing lanes allows for competitive swimming. Acoustic absorbers hanging over the pool are also used for signs (photographer: Martin Charles).*

Fig. 3.8   *Entrance foyer with changing-rooms and stair on left and cafeteria on right; the pool is beyond the planters and screen (photographer: Martin Charles).*

Fig. 3.9   *The south-facing filter plant room. Ozone is used as a disinfectant allowing the air withdrawn from the pool area to be dehumidified and recirculated (up to 80 per cent under normal use) (photographer: Martin Charles).*

3.5

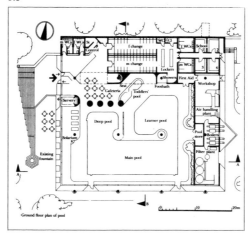

3.6

3.7

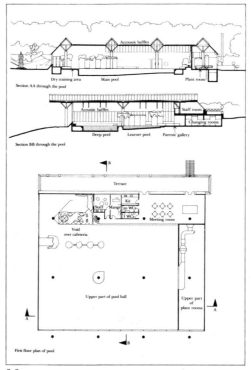

3,6

3.8

3.9

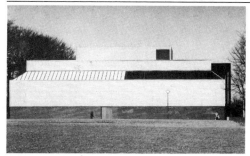

3.10

3.12

3.11

3.13

3.15

3.14

3.16

Fig. 3.10   The east side of the Bury St Edmunds Sports Centre (see plan). Note angled high-level fenestration glazed with solar control safety glass; this is available in a wide range of percentage light transmissions some of which have been deployed in the building according to the function and orientation of each area (photographer: Martin Charles).

Fig. 3.11   Plans and section a–a.

Fig. 3.12   Learner pool with continuous steps along one side. The sloping ceiling reflects light inwards very efficiently (photographer: Martin Charles).

Fig. 3.13   Main pool seen from the east end. Refreshment and viewing areas are behind the glazed screen on first floor level (photographer: Martin Charles).

Fig. 3.14   Comfortable and popular viewing area, with restaurant and bar nearby, overlooks the main pool on the left (photographer: Martin Charles).

Fig. 3.15   Sports hall with spectator viewing areas on two levels (photographer: Martin Charles).

Fig. 3.16   Practice halls and other spaces (for example, the licensed area) are used during the day for a large variety of courses for the young, old and handicapped (photographer: Martin Charles).

Fig. 3.17   Rectangular-shaped 33.3 m long pool suitable for competitive swimming (six-lane width) with both permanent spectator seating (left) and an informal high-level viewing gallery. A separate learner pool is screened by the dwarf wall at the far (shallow) end (photographer: Dennis Wompra).

Fig. 3.18   Another example of a rectangular pool for competitive swimming with some fixed seating at pool level – Bury St Edmunds Sports Centre. See also Figs. 3.10–3.16 (photographer: Martin Charles).

Fig. 3.19   Large areas of shallow water, waves, waterfalls, plastic 'rocks' and tropical plants – some of the essential ingredients for a leisure-type pool. Note module at balcony level which contains control desk with tape deck, microphone, telephone, lighting switches and wave-machine controls (photographer: Tony Whitley).

Fig. 3.20   This leisure pool incorporates a 25 m long area, between parallel end walls, which can be used for training and competitive swimming. The racing lane markings can be seen on the floor beyond the glass-fibre whale (photographer: Keith Gibson).

Fig. 3.21   Many leisure pools are designed with large areas of glazing to provide natural lighting. Solar heat gain/loss can be a major problem (photographer: Bill Toomey).

Fig. 3.22   An example of a completely artificially lit leisure pool. The various forms of lighting (for example, recessed ceiling fittings, the hanging 'suns', etc.) can be used to create different effects (photographer: Keith Gibson).

3.17

3.18

3.19

3.20

3.21

3.22

3.23

3.24

3.25

3.26

3.27

Fig. 3.23   *Typical beach-type edge to a leisure pool with water depth varying to zero up a gentle slope. This type of edge is needed for wave machines (photographer: Keith Gibson).*

Fig. 3.24   *Typical level deck edge detail with continuous cover grille on overflow channel. Note non-slip flooring used on pool surround (photographer: Keith Gibson).*

Fig. 3.25   *At specialised pools (for example, those used for hydrotherapy) provision may need to be made for hydraulic or mechanically operated hoists. Such expensive and sophisticated equipment is not normally used in public pools (Mecanaids).*

Fig. 3.26   *The roof is raised over the 10 m diving tower and the diving pool only to provide the required height rather than have an unnecessarily high roof over the whole swimming hall.*

Fig. 3.27   *Spectators view this diving tower against a background of glazing making it very difficult to see the divers properly. Diving should ideally be viewed against a solid background (photographer: H. Heldersberger).*

Fig. 3.28   *Blind box-type multi-purpose hall from which natural light is completely omitted. Note fluorescent light fittings mounted parallel to long sides of badminton courts: the fittings should be above or outside the side lines (photographer: Colin Curwood).*

Fig. 3.29   *A troughed ceiling with continuous rooflights and fluorescent light fittings helps to provide relatively glare-free natural and artificial lighting (photographer: Martin Charles).*

Fig. 3.30   *Sports hall in which the clerestory windows have been painted and the side wall windows fitted with curtains to cut out glare.*

Figs. 3.31–3.35   *Various activities taking place in large multi-purpose sports halls. Note use of curtains, netting, etc., to screen and divide the space for different activities to take place concurrently (photographers: Bill Toomey – Fig. 3.32; Martin Charles – Fig. 3.33; Henk Snoek – Fig. 3.34; Peter Baistow – Fig. 3.35).*

3.28

3.29

3.30

3.31

3.32

3.33

3.34

3.35

3.36

3.37

3.38

3.39

Fig. 3.36   *Main and ancillary halls placed side by side. Sharp corner of dividing wall is potentially dangerous. Ideally all corners should be rounded.*

Fig. 3.37   *Ancillary hall containing a climbing-wall. Full height room-divider is used to provide two separate spaces (photographer: Bill Toomey).*

Fig. 3.38   *Judo, karate, table tennis and various other activities are frequently accommodated in an ancillary hall, freeing the main hall for sports requiring large spaces (photographer: Martin Charles).*

Fig. 3.39   *An ancillary hall used for movement and dance activities should be provided with a reasonably large area of wall-mounted mirror and barres. Windows providing a view to the outside help to create a pleasant atmosphere.*

Figs. 3.40–3.42 *Projectile hall used primarily for archery, shooting, cricket and golf (photographers: Bill Toomey – Fig. 3.40; John Donat – Figs. 3.41, 3.42).*

Fig. 3.43 *A small ice rink (600 m² ice pad) with bright, cheerful atmosphere which is part of a comprehensive school with extensive community facilities (photographer: Martin Charles).*

Fig. 3.44 *Large ice rink. Note the boards and protective end screens used for ice hockey.*

Fig. 3.45 *Skating on a synthetic ice surface in a multi-purpose hall.*

Figs. 3.46 and 3.47 *Two different forms of climbing-wall (photographer: Henk Snoek – Fig. 3.47).*

3.40

3.41

3.42

3.43

3.44

3.45

3.46

3.47

3.48

3.49

3.50

3.51

3.52

3.53

3.54

3.55

Fig. 3.48   *Weight training room viewed from circulation space. Carpeted floor, suspended ceiling, curtains and tungsten lighting make this a pleasant space for keep-fit, as well as the more serious athletic and weight lifting exercises (photographer: Jo Reid).*

Fig. 3.49   *Typical weight training room with multi-station weight training apparatus (photographer: Martin Charles).*

Fig. 3.50   *Glass back wall to squash court with permanent raked seating behind (photographer: John Donat).*

Fig. 3.51   *Glass back wall and special balcony for referee or coach (photographer: Philip Sayer).*

Fig. 3.52   *Glass walls on three sides of the court. Twin-Vue glass is used – this allows spectators to see through the glass which, coupled with high light intensity on the playing side, gives a one-way characteristic enabling players to locate the wall and judge the speed and position of the ball (Ellis Pearson Glasswalls).*

Fig. 3.53   *Specialist squash club building with informal viewing area behind the glass back wall of the courts (photographer: Dave Bower).*

Fig. 3.54   *Indoor bowling green with bank and surround on same level.*

Fig. 3.55   *Surround to this indoor green is on same level as ditch. Note opening in bank on long side to allow access for the disabled (photographer: Jo Reid).*

Figs. 3.56 *and* 3.57 *Drama workshop with lighting grid and curtained stage area (photographer: Martin Charles).*

Fig. 3.58 *Multi-purpose craft area with large windows for natural lighting and outside door for delivery of materials (photographer: Martin Charles).*

Fig. 3.59 *Crèche. If space is to be used for other functions, for example as a committee/club room, adequate storage must be provided for tables, chairs, tarpaulins (for protecting the carpeted floor), toys, etc. (photographer: Martin Charles).*

Figs. 3.60 *and* 3.61 *Two examples of informal viewing galleries linked to refreshment facilities. Note the netting screen between the viewing gallery and the sports hall in Fig. 3.60 (photographers: Bill Toomey – Fig. 3.60; de Burgh Galwey – Fig. 3.61).*

3.56

3.57

3.58

3.59

3.60

3.61

3.62

3.63

Figs. 3.62 *and* 3.63 *Sophisticated refreshment and social areas are becoming more commonplace in sports and recreation centres and the inclusion of licensed bars (such as these two examples), coffee bars and cafeterias contributes not only towards fostering a more congenial atmosphere but also to the income of the centre (photographers: John Donat – Fig. 3.62; Dave Bower – Fig. 3.63).*

Figs. 3.64–3.67 *Four examples of reception/central control areas. Entry turnstiles are usually controlled by a switch from the reception counter. If turnstiles are used an alternative entry point must be provided for wheelchair users and the ambulant disabled (photographers: Sam Lambert – Fig. 3.64; Keith Gibson – Fig. 3.65. Figs. 3.66 and 3.67 supplied by Randalls of Paddington).*

3.64

3.66

3.65

3.67

Fig. 3.68   *A clear, simple and neat system of interrelated signs to identify, direct and inform must be planned for the entrance foyer, circulation routes and main activity areas (photographer: Colin Curwood).*

Fig. 3.69   *One or more franchise elements – shop, hairdresser, sauna – may be included, often located adjacent to the entrance/reception area. The shop in this example is part of a squash club with the glasswall courts arranged around it and a central bar (photographer: Mike Craven).*

Figs. 3.70 *and* 3.71   *Entry control systems are used in many sports and leisure centres at points where secondary control is required – for example, entrances/exits to changing-rooms, etc. These units may be either coin or token operated (Randalls of Paddington).*

Fig. 3.72   *Typical changing-room with communal changing on benches and some provision for individual cubicles. Clothes are stored in lockers which may be coin operated (Randalls of Paddington).*

Fig. 3.73   *Lockers for dry sports often need to be larger to accommodate winter clothes and bulky items such as sports bags (Randalls of Paddington).*

3.69

3.68

3.70

3.71

3.72

3.73

3.74

3.75

3.77

3.78

3.76

3.79

3.80

Fig. 3.74 *Open plan changing – often in a lockable room; possibly a 'buffer' or 'interchange' room – is commonly provided for team and/or school use (Amdega).*

Fig. 3.75 *Central basket storage area which requires staff supervision (photographer: Bill Toomey).*

Fig. 3.76 *There should ideally be a drying off (or towelling) area between the showers and the change room (photographer: Simo Rista).*

Fig. 3.77 *The sauna may be custom designed for the project in question or a prefabricated unit of either panel or log (as in this example) construction. When space and finance permits two or more smaller saunas, maintained at different temperatures, is an ideal solution rather than one large unit (Norpe-Saunas of Finland).*

Figs. 3.78 and 3.79 *Although basically very simple, there are a few important requirements that must be adhered to if the hot room is to be a genuine sauna. Economics of prefabrication obviously impose limits to what can be accomplished and the model that meets all requirements has yet to be devised. The cost of different models must be weighed against the shortcomings that each will certainly have. The interior of a prefabricated panel sauna (Fig. 3.78); the interior of a custom built sauna (Fig. 3.79) (Fig. 3.78 – Nordic Saunas).*

Fig. 3.80 *Typical solarium or sunbed. These units are fitted with UVA tubes and, usually, with cooling fans to give a pleasant bathing temperature and to ensure optimum efficiency of the tubes. Approximate size 2–2.25 m long × 0.6–1 m wide (Nordic Saunas).*

Fig. 3.81   *Various synthetic surfaces are being widely used in multi-purpose sports halls. They are generally suitable for all normal sports and games and can accommodate various non-sporting activities. The seamless neoprene-rubber composite floor illustrated can have the games lines included in the system underneath the final clear resin coat (Dex-O-Tex).*

Fig. 3.82   *The large number of different activities that a multi-purpose sports hall has to accommodate can require an almost bewildering array of court markings. Where possible, markings for the different sports should be of distinctive colours. Lines may be of inlay strips, marking paints or self-adhesive tapes (photographer: Peter Baistow).*

Figs. 3.83 and 3.84   *Two views of the same sports hall. Note the effectiveness of the V-shaped ceiling baffles in cutting out glare from the rooflights and fluorescent fittings when viewed at right-angles (Fig. 3.83). They are less effective when play is parallel with the baffles (Fig. 3.84) (photographers: Allan Hurst – Fig. 3.83; Keith Gibson – Fig. 3.84).*

Fig. 3.85   *Bleacher seating stored beneath a balcony acting as a 'door' to a store.*

3.82

3.81

3.83

3.84

3.85

3.86

3.87

3.88

3.89

Fig. 3.86   *Typical retractable bleacher seating (photograph: Reith and Partners).*

Figs. 3.87 and 3.88   *Portable all-purpose folding chairs which can be linked by brackets allowing ganging of chairs in perfect alignment. Chairs may be stored on a variety of standard trolleys – up to 108 (depending on the model) can be stored on the trolley illustrated in Fig. 3.88. Approximate size when loaded: 1.75 m long × 0.75– 1.25 m wide × 2 m high (Sandler Seating).*

Fig. 3.89   *A glass squash wall which opens in the middle and swings back like two large gates allowing the court to be used for other activities (Ellis Pearson Glasswalls).*

A.4 The main consultants

a. Architects

Only persons appropriately qualified and registered under the Architects' Registration Acts may use the title architect. Although this may be a guarantee of a certain level of competence, it is certainly no more than that. Architects vary greatly in their outlook and approach: some are general practitioners, others are specialists; some are artists, others are businessmen. It is, therefore, very important for a client to find the right architect for the specific project in question.

One way of doing this is by approaching the Clients' Advisory Service of the RIBA (see 'Professional bodies' below) for advice. When the field has been narrowed to a few firms it is wise to visit each one to meet and talk to the partners and to see how each office is organised as well as examples of the firm's work before making a final decision.

In the USA there is a new way of matching client with designer: the public sector has recently been obliged by legislation to advertise its requirements for architectural services to which interested architects may respond. As a result the American Institute of Architects has been forced to abandon its prohibition of competitive bidding for projects by member practices. Without radical changes in Government policy this could not happen in the UK.

Responsibilities and services

The architect's primary professional responsibility is to act as the client's adviser and additionally to administer the building contract fairly between client and contractor. Architects generally provide a variety of services to meet the special requirements of their clients. The work normally undertaken during the course of a building project is described by the RIBA as 'basic services' and it may be summarised as follows (the work described is usually undertaken together with other appointed consultants):

1   Preliminary services which include: discussing, reviewing and evaluating the client's brief; providing advice on how to proceed and on the need for other consultants' services; site visit and initial appraisal; and preparation of outline timetable.
2   Analysis of requirements and preparation of feasibility studies.
3   Outline proposals and an estimate of construction cost for the client's preliminary approval.
4   Development of a scheme design together with cost estimate; attending to applications for planning permission.
5   Detail design and co-ordination of design work done by other consultants and specialists; attending to applications for building approvals.
6   Advising on and arranging for tenders and contract.
7   Contract administration and site supervision up to completion of the works.

Details of these and other services which architects may be called upon to provide, either to augment the basic services or as a separate service, for example, the preparation of the brief (which in many cases is considered an additional service) can be obtained from the RIBA.

Fees

Until recently architects' fees were based on a set of standard mandatory figures prepared by the RIBA. Various fee options are now available and which is used depends on factors including the service to be provided, the size and type of project and negotiations between client and architect. The three basic options used are:

1   Percentage of total construction cost. The RIBA has separate recommended fee scales for new works and works to existing buildings. These consist of sliding scales for different classes of work – the higher the cost of the project and the less complex the building type, the lower the percentage.
2   Time charges based on hourly rates for principals and other technical staff.
3   In certain cases architect and client may agree on a lump sum.

Professional bodies

The Royal Institute of British Architects (RIBA)
66 Portland Place
London W1N 4AD
Tel. 01-580 5533

The Royal Incorporation of Architects in Scotland (RIAS)
15 Rutland Square
Edinburgh EH1 2BE
Tel. 031-229 7205

The Royal Society of Ulster Architects
2 Mount Charles
Belfast BT7 1NZ

The American Institute of Architects
1735 New York Avenue, NW.
Washington DC 20006

Most architectural firms in the UK are members of RIBA and are governed by its code of professional conduct. The services which can be provided by architects, the conditions of appointment and the scale of fees charged by them for particular services are described in *Architect's Appointment* and in the *Directory of Practices* which also includes the names and addresses of member practices and the types of work they undertake. These and other publications produced by RIBA are available from their bookshop at the London address. The Institute provides a client's advisory service. Their library contains a comprehensive collection of publications on architecture and is open to the general public for reference.

b.   Building surveyors

Services

A chartered building surveyor is qualified by examination and experience as a member of the Royal Institution of Chartered Surveyors, and can provide an advisory or consultancy service on various aspects of the construction and economics of buildings. This includes:

1   the diagnosis of building defects and advice on remedial work;
2   the planning and implementation of maintenance work;
3   project management; and
4   structural surveys of all types of property.

Fees

Fees are often based on the time involved but in some cases, such as the supervision of building work, it may be based on a percentage of the overall cost of the project. The Royal Institution of Chartered Surveyors publishes *Conditions of Engagement for Building Surveying Services* which sets out in detail the type of work carried out. Potential clients should consult this publication and a fee for the service to be provided should be agreed prior to instructions being given.

Professional body

The Royal Institution of Chartered Surveyors (RICS)
12 Great George Street
Parliament Square
London SW1P 3AD
Tel. 01-222 7000
and
7 Manor Place
Edinburgh EH3 7DN
Tel. 031-225 7078

c. Engineers

Services

There are two main groups of engineers: civil and structural, and services engineers. The first group form part of the design team to assist with the design and calculations for elements such as foundations, retaining walls, columns, beams, slabs and roofs whether these are of reinforced concrete, steel or timber. On some projects (for example, those consisting largely of structural elements) the engineer may be employed as the principal designer.

Services engineers are appointed as members of the design team to assist with the design of environmental control aspects such as lighting, heating and air-conditioning, and mechanical services. As these items can represent a high proportion of building costs, the appointment of the required consultants at an early enough stage for them to participate in the briefing process and feasibility studies is to be recommended.

Fees

For details of fees in relation to services provided contact the Association of Consulting Engineers or the appropriate institution.

Professional bodies

The Association of Consulting Engineers
1st Floor
Alliance House
12 Caxton Street
London SW1H 0QL
Tel. 01-222 6557
This is a professional association of independent consulting engineers. It provides an advisory service and, if requested to do so, will nominate suitable members for particular purposes. Publications are produced describing the services provided by consulting engineers, the conditions of engagement and the scale of fees.

The Chartered Institution of Building Services
Delta House
222 Balham High Road
London SW12 9BS
Tel. 01-675 5211
The Institution promotes the science and practice of heating, ventilation, air-conditioning, domestic hot water engineering and all other building services. Enquiry and advisory services are available.

The American Institute of Consulting Engineers
345 E 47th Street
New York
NY 10017

d. Interior designers

Services

These professionals generally provide the same design and technical services that an architect provides but restrict their work to interiors only.

An interior designer may work on a project in association with other professionals (as part of a design team), or may in certain cases (non-structural refurbishment) be the sole consultant. In all cases the interior designer may be appointed by agreement for one or more of the following progressive stages:

1 A study of the client's requirements and the scope of work; ascertaining feasibility and advising on the need for other specialist consultants. The preparation of preliminary proposal including initial assessment of cost and programme.

2 The preparation of detailed proposals and the necessary working drawings and specifications required for determining the contract cost. The invitation of tenders from approved contractors.

3 The submission of a report on tenders; and advising on the selection of contractors, etc.; supervision of the contract.

An interior design consultant may also be commissioned in an advisory capacity or for part of the whole normal service including the preparation of feasibility studies and reports, detail surveys, etc.

Fees

There are three primary ways in which consultancy services are charged:

1 a percentage basis where an agreed percentage figure (usually on a sliding scale and between 15-10 or less per cent) is applied to the whole cost of the works plus remuneration for expenses;

2 a time basis where agreed time rates are levied plus expenses (small jobs are usually done on this basis); or

3 a lump sum basis where a total fee is agreed for the services specified.

Professional bodies

The British Institute of Interior Design
Lenton Lodge
Wollaton Hall Drive
Nottingham NG8 1AF
Tel. 0602-701205

This is a professional organisation of interior designers, designers in related disciplines, crafts persons/designers and persons who provide a service in one or more specific areas within the interior environment. The Institute can supply details of services, fee scales, etc., and will supply clients with a short list of interior designers of appropriate experience for specific projects.

The American Institute of Interior Designers
730 5th Avenue
New York
NY 10019

e.   Landscape consultants

The term landscape consultant refers to the following three groups of professionals:
1   Landscape architects who are trained in the planning and design of all types of outdoor spaces. They use knowledge of the natural elements of the landscape, its materials and components, to create the spatial and aesthetic elements of the new environment. Many practitioners are also qualified in other disciplines such as horticulture, planning or architecture. They may develop projects into contracts and supervise their execution on site.
2   Landscape scientists who are concerned with the physical and biological principles and processes which underlie the planning, design and management of natural resources. They have the ability to relate their scientific knowledge to the practical problems of landscape work which can range from small-scale site surveys to ecological assessments. Landscape scientists usually have a science background such as ecology, often with specialist skills such as soil science, hydrology or botany.
3   Landscape managers are specialists employing management techniques in the long-term care and development of new and existing landscapes. They usually have a degree in horticulture, forestry or agriculture together with further training in land management or other related disciplines.

Services
The landscape consultant's work involves both the existing landscape and the design and implementation of new landscapes and is generally associated with other professionals such as architects, planners, ecologists and engineers. The scale of work undertaken can vary considerably from designing a small courtyard or settings for all kinds of buildings to designing recreation facilities and preparing landscape plans for large areas.
The services provided may take the form of purely advisory work or may include surveys, appraisal, implementation and management. When engaged on a typical commission related to building work the landscape consultant may perform some, or all, of the following services:
1   the appraisal of site conditions;
2   the survey of the site to provide accurate information about the nature of the land and soil, including the existing features, the condition and lifespan of trees and shrubs, and the types of plants already growing or likely to grow;
3   the preparation of preliminary sketch plans and approximate estimates for the client's approval;

4 the preparation of all drawings and specifications required for the execution of the work;

5 the preparation of contract documents (other than bills of quantities); also obtaining and advising on tenders;

6 the administration of the contract and supervision of the work on site;

7 checking and certifying accounts (but not measurement and valuation of the work); and

8 the submission of plans for necessary approvals by public bodies.

Fees

There are two main methods of determining remuneration: on the time basis or on the percentage basis, with reinbursement for expenses being added to the fee in both cases. Full details may be obtained from the Landscape Institute.

The percentage basis is only applied to a contract costing £10,000 and over and is calculated from two components: a percentage figure is read off a graph against the cost of the project (that is, the higher the project cost the lower the percentage). This figure is the 'norm' which is adjusted by a coefficient based on either the form of contract or the type of job (and therefore its complexity). Some services (for example, site surveys) are specifically excluded from those within the percentage 'norm' and are charged for additionally on a time basis or negotiated sum.

Professional bodies

The Landscape Institute
12 Carlton House Terrace
London SW1Y 5AH
Tel. 01-839 4044
The Institute can provide information on conditions of engagement and professional charges and will nominate practices for commissions at the request of clients. It operates a reference library and publishes a quarterly journal, *Landscape Design*, which is available to non-members on subscription.
The American Institute of Landscape Architects
501 E San Juan Avenue
Phoenix
A285012

f. Land surveyors

Services

In a world of rapidly changing technology, the services offered by land surveyors are constantly adapting and expanding to meet the needs of a wide variety of clients. The major advisory and/or consultancy services offered to those involved in new construction work include:

1 property boundary surveys;

2 area or site surveying;

3 architectural surveys, to record new and existing buildings in plan, by section or in elevation;

4 setting out of building and construction work; and

5 aerial photography and photogrammetry – orthophotomaps or the recording of historic buildings and monuments etc.

Fees

There is no fee scale for land surveying services and information on ranges of fees for specific services may be obtained from the Royal Institution of Chartered Surveyors or directly from member firms.

Professional body

The Royal Institution of Chartered Surveyors (RICS)
12 Great George Street
Parliament Square
London SW1P 3AD
Tel. 01-222 7000
and
7 Manor Place
Edinburgh EH3 7DN
Tel. 031-225 7078

The Institution has an information centre which runs a nomination service for clients and will always give guidance on services offered or transfer a client to the appropriate divisional secretary. Various publications are available including the *Directory of Land and Hydrographic Survey Services in the United Kingdom.*

g. Quantity surveyors

Services

The quantity surveyor is the expert professional trained to assist clients and architects with construction costs, construction management and construction communications. This consultant is an important member of the briefing and design team and should be appointed at an early stage to provide some, or all, of the following services:

1 preliminary cost advice including recommendations on most economical layout, materials and methods of construction; also estimates of future maintenance and running costs;

2 estimates of the costs of alternative proposals;

3 cost planning – a specialist technique used to help all the members of the design team to arrive jointly at practical designs for a specific project and stay within the agreed budget. Also assessment of the cost implications of changes;

4 advising on contractual methods;

5 preparing bills of quantities which are used for competitive tendering and as an

important element if effective cost control during construction;

6 negotiating tenders for projects planned from the outset with a single contractor. It is advisable to consider appointing an independent quantity surveyor for advise on the financial and contractual aspects when embarking on a package deal;

7 financial management and valuing of work during construction; and

8 preparing final accounts, statements of expenditure for tax or accountancy purposes etc.

Fees

Recommended scales of fees related to the cost and complexity of the project are published by RICS. Chartered quantity surveyors will always provide estimates of their fees and RICS will give advice when necessary.

Professional body

The Royal Institution of Chartered Surveyors (RICS)
12 Great George Street
Parliament Square
London SW1P 3AD
Tel. 01-222 7000
and
7 Manor Place
Edinburgh EH3 7DN
Tel. 031-225 7078
The Institution has an information centre which runs a nomination service for clients and will always give guidance on services offered or transfer a client to the appropriate divisional secretary. Various publications are available including leaflets describing the main services offered, and package contracts.

A.5 Briefing and design methods

There are a number of briefing and design methods which can be used to help produce different kinds of information (see Fig. A.1). Each of these techniques or tools is a separate activity for collecting, exploring, communicating, analysing, organising or evaluating information and ideas, and it is a question of not only determining whether one or more of them will be appropriate to a specific project, but also matching them with information needs. The methods used for a particular design situation will depend, amongst other things, on the people involved, on the stage one is at, on what is already known and on what one is trying to find out.

A few of the most basic, and perhaps more useful, methods are described here in broad outline. For more detailed information refer to Appendix A.1.a:

a. Literature search

To locate and retrieve published information which will not only help to lay the foundation for further investigation and for preliminary conclusions, but will also provide some of the required design data.

1 Identify the purposes for which the information is required and ascertain priorities.

2 Determine the degree of detail required – bare essentials may be sufficient initially.

3 Identify likely sources of reliable, up-to-date and relevant information. In many cases (for example, where those involved have previous experience of the relevant building type) the process may simply involve updating knowledge from literature already available in one's own library.

Literature search can be time-consuming. It is advisable to determine a timetable taking into account, not only by when the information will be required, but also a deadline beyond which the search will be discontinued. The penalty of insufficient information at a given time must be balanced against the cost of obtaining it.

Fig. A.1 *Chart indicating some of the many methods that can be employed during the briefing and design process as well as the kinds of actions for which they may be used (● = primary use, ○ = secondary use). The methods in heavy type are described in outline in this Appendix.*

Indicates method which is generally a group activity

Indicates method which generally involves users

Methods	Kinds of action / categories of information			
	Exploring design situations and/or data gathering	Searching for or generating ideas	Exploring problem structure (analysis & organisation)	Evaluation
Stating objectives	●			
Literature search	●	○		
Interview	●	○		
Questionnaire	●	○		
Observation	●	○		
Visit/study existing buildings	●	○		
Data logs	●		○	
Standardised data forms	●		●	
Brainstorming		●	○	
Synectics		●	○	
Role playing		●	○	
Gaming		●	○	
Interaction matrix			●	
Correlation diagrams			●	
Functional innovation			●	
Pattern language	○	●	●	○
Classification			●	
Checklists	●		○	●
Selecting criteria				●
Ranking and weighting				●
Cost planning			●	
Life cycle cost analysis			●	●
Value analysis			●	●
Cost benefit analysis			●	●
Energy accounting			●	○
Post occupancy appraisal				●

The choice of sources and the applicability of data being collected must be continuously evaluated. Literature search should be stopped as soon as sufficient useful data to answer the stated questions has been gathered. Accurate references should be kept of all publications that are found to be useful for easy retrieval at a later date, and collected data should be stored in a flexible way so that new information can be readily added.

b. Interviews

This is the most common and direct method of obtaining specific and detailed information from clients and users. Interviews serve the same purpose as questionnaires but have the advantage of direct and immediate interaction between interviewer and client or user.

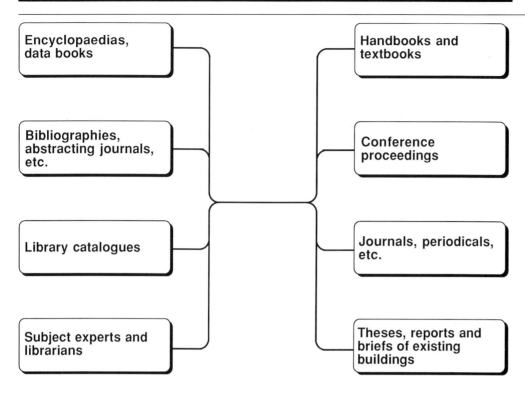

Fig. A.2 *Sources of information.*

Encyclopaedias, data books	Handbooks and textbooks
Bibliographies, abstracting journals, etc.	Conference proceedings
Library catalogues	Journals, periodicals, etc.
Subject experts and librarians	Theses, reports and briefs of existing buildings

Interviews may be unstructured or structured. The former – in which no predetermined format is used – tends to be exploratory in nature and is often employed with the aim of gaining a general understanding of a problem or situation; and also of identifying the right questions to include in a questionnaire or structured interview. Structured interviews, on the other hand, follow a pre-arranged format in order to generate quick responses to specific questions.

1 Identify the kinds of information needed.
2 Identify the different types of people involved in the user situations that require exploration: client, managers, operators, consumers, etc. Each type will usually have different impressions, needs, attitudes, values, preferences and problems, some of which will almost certainly be in conflict with those of the other types or groups.
3 Establish contact with and obtain the co-operation of the various groups involved.
4 Prepare a set of questions or a checklist: it is only common sense to obtain expert advice.
5 Decide who will be interviewed and make the necessary arrangements. Allow sufficient time for the predetermined questions to be answered and/or for free discussion.
6 Those interviewed should be allowed to talk spontaneously about any aspects of the activities in which they are involved that seem important to them, and encouraged to expand on those which are particularly relevant to the

design situation being explored. This should be possible even in a structured interview.

7   Responses, comments and suggestions must be accurately recorded together with relevant circumstantial information: the ages, sex and expertise of those interviewed, etc.

8   It is generally useful for the interviewer to have some experience of the actual user-situation being explored, and the interviews may be preceded, or followed up, by one of the observation techniques.

9   Interviewers should try to remain neutral and remember that the views and interests of the *interviewee* are being sought. (Interviewers may well have to listen to views with which they totally disagree and must not get carried away by their own points of view.)

c.   Questionnaire

This serves basically the same purpose as an interview – of which it may form part – but takes the form of a written set of questions which generally require a written response. It is used to obtain a variety of usable information from large numbers of people.

1   Identify the kinds of information needed to meet specific objectives.
2   Identify the different types/groups of people involved and consider which would be most helpful in obtaining the information required.
3   Consider the types of questions which will be most suitable to get the information required: factual, informative, opinion/attitude and/or self-perception. Also consider how the answers are to be analysed.
4   Consider the form in which answers are to be given: questions can be unstructured – open-ended, encouraging descriptions of likes, dislikes, attitudes, values, behaviour and settings – or can require a fixed response: choice between two possibilities (yes/no; good/bad, etc.), multiple choice or ranking of set of alternatives. Although the fixed response method is obviously easier to analyse and to feed into a computer, both types of questions are often used in a single questionnaire.

When formulating questions, keep in mind that they should be short and use language that makes the meaning clear to all respondents. They should be free from any possible bias (assumptions and prejudices of the questioner), and should elicit definite, short, simple and useful answers.

Consider the design of the questionnaire: it should be laid out so that it is easy to understand and use, and does not take too long to complete. The following sequence, with questions designed to flow naturally from one to the next, is widely used:

1   Short introduction: explanation of purpose and instructions.
2   Easy-to-answer preliminary questions.
3   The main questions or body of the questionnaire.
4   Questions eliciting personal data.

Establish how the questionnaire is to be circulated, for example, in interviews, by post or at a meeting. If sent by post an accompanying explanatory letter should be enclosed.

It is essential, if the exercise is to have any validity, to draw up and circulate a pilot questionnaire to test the questions and answers, and the method of analysis, before drafting the final document.

d. Observation

It is often helpful – and sometimes essential – for designers to expose themselves to the complexities of the real situation they are designing for. The various observation techniques can be employed to get useful information about people's behaviour in a specific environment/setting: patterns of behaviour and use, space requirements and relationships, the use of furniture and equipment, dysfunction, etc. Other methods (for example, interviews) will be needed to get information on the users' opinions and attitudes.

1 Identify the kinds of information needed, for example, details of the activities that take place – the different kinds as well as their frequency, duration and sequence; physical and other characteristics of the space or setting; details of the various interactions among users and between them and the setting; general data on the users involved.

2 Consider whether the study will be exploratory – to gain a general understanding; or structured – to collect specific detailed information.

3 Identify the various types of users and settings involved and consider which are to be observed: in the case of data collection for an airport design, for example, one will need to know something about the behaviour/use patterns of not only travellers but also visitors, flight crews, ground staff, administrators, etc.

4 Determine what method(s) will be used:

— Direct unobtrusive observation. This may be best if users are likely to modify their actions when knowing they are being watched.

— Direct observation with the co-operation of users. It is sometimes useful to observe not only experienced users but also volunteers inexperienced in the use of the space or setting, noting their reactions and difficulties while attempting to achieve a predetermined objective.

— Participation by the observer: several sessions may be required to experience different user situations/perspectives.

— Other: tracking, behaviour-mapping, etc. See Appendix A.1.a: Jones[1], Palmer[2], Sanoff[4] and Cross & Roy.

5 Obtain the necessary permission and/or co-operation needed to carry out the proposed study.

6 Decide how data – actions, difficulties, problems, impressions, ideas, etc. – will be recorded. Consider the possibility of using mechanical methods such as tape recording, still or time-lapse photography, videotaping or cine-filming.

Note: It must be pointed out that interviews, questionnaires and observations are research-based methods on which there is a great deal written and still some controversy. Even those trained in these methods can make mistakes and can draw the wrong conclusions from the data collected. One must, therefore, not only get expert help/advice, but also remember that while the results from these methods may give good indications of attitudes, they should be treated circumspectly and certainly not as 'the answer'.

e.   Visit/study existing buildings

Before embarking on a project, a great deal can be learnt by architect, client and selected users through visits to similar organisations and buildings. There is no better way to keep abreast of new developments and obtain an insight into the problems of a particular building type, while also becoming aware of, experiencing and evaluating the many alternative solutions. While a careful study of the literature of the subject is a good introduction it is not, generally speaking, by itself sufficient.

1   Go through published information on the building type in question (in architectural journals and other professional publications).
2   Draw up a list of possible buildings to visit. When making a final selection, remember:
—   It is useful to visit a few buildings that will be reasonably comparable in size and character to the one being planned and, ideally, those that offer a wide range of alternative approaches in terms of layout, construction, finishes and equipment.
—   Buildings which appear to be most attractive in photographs and which are widely publicised, are not necessarily the ones that function best for occupants and users. Although much can be learned from both good and bad examples, the greater number of successful solutions one can visit the better.
—   Do not attempt to visit too many buildings. It is generally advisable to keep the number down to between six and eight that can be examined carefully enough to make the exercise worthwhile.
3   Decide who will go on the visits: client, architect, selected staff and/or users. A small group made up of people with different backgrounds will provide a variety of points of view. If a specialist building consultant has been appointed his presence will be helpful as he will be able to point out satisfactory solutions of problems as well as failures. This consultant would almost certainly be able to suggest some buildings worth visiting.
4   Prepare a programme for the proposed visits allowing enough time (between a half and a full day) to study each building, see visual demonstrations and ask questions. Contact the organisations in question to arrange for the visits and for appointments with the people who should be seen.

5 Draw up a checklist of things to be looked at, points to be discussed and questions to which answers are needed:

— How was the project organised: Who prepared the brief? What sort of consultants were used? Who made various design decisions and why were they made? What would be changed with hindsight?

— Who uses the building and what kinds of functions does it house? What were the user requirements and client objectives? How well are these met by the building in question?

— How were decisions made about the interior design? What space standards were used? Is it easy to find one's way about? Are layouts of spaces satisfactory or unacceptable? Do some areas seem unduly congested and are there others where space is obviously wasted?

— What system is used – structural grid, depth of spaces, etc. – and how well does this suit the functions? What is the relationship of service ducts and vertical circulation to the structure? What are the ceiling heights? Are they satisfactory for the various activities involved? How practical are the materials used for floors, walls and ceilings in terms of function, quality, appearance, maintenance, sound and cost?

— What form of lighting is used and is the quality of light satisfactory for the tasks to be performed? What system is used to provide power/communication outlets? How flexible is it? What were the acoustic criteria? Is there any sound disturbance?

— What kinds of furniture and equipment are used? How were they selected? How well do they meet the criteria of function, flexibility, quality, appearance, maintenance and cost?

— To what extent has flexibility/adaptability and possible future extension been provided for? How has it been done?

— What methods will be used to collect the data required: by interviewing those involved in the briefing, by talking to staff, from observation, etc?

6 Take notes during each visit. These will be helpful during subsequent discussions and for the preparation of a written report which is a useful way of organising information and ideas, and of making them available to others. It may be worthwhile taking photographs during visits to illustrate, and remind one of, specific points.

7 If it is not possible to visit some important buildings they should at least be carefully examined, ideally by studying the original brief and, if at all possible, any published post-occupancy appraisal (or evaluation as it is called in the USA). Where such material is available it is well worth studying even if the building has been visited as it provides useful supplementary information.

Post-occupancy appraisal, especially from clients' and users' points of view, has great value both as a first step in the development of a building brief – it offers the potential for obtaining the type of feedback needed to avoid past mistakes and improve the design process – and as a final step in assessing user satisfaction when it may be used for fine-tuning of the building. Although there is a growing awareness of the need for this type of study, there is at present relatively little published material available. Appraisals published in the architectural press, which range from very general descriptions to detailed case studies, do not generally attempt to examine how users relate to the building and the reasons why the building may be satisfactory or have failed in use.

f. Standardised data forms

These are used to collect, record and organise various types of routine or repetitive data (room requirements, descriptions of existing facilities, user activities, energy consumption, etc.). They are an ideal way of presenting detailed design information consistently for each space, system or activity in a building brief.

1 Identify the type of data that is to be collected and recorded, for example, requirements for each of the spaces in the building.
2 Determine the various categories of information that are needed, for example, activities/functions to be performed in the area, number of occupants/ users, furniture and equipment, floor area, relationship to other spaces, environmental conditions, special finishes.
3 Decide on the most suitable method of recording the different types of data and prepare a layout for the form accordingly, for example, form may allow clocks within which the necessary data is filled in or may be organised as a checklist. Where possible the form should be kept to a single sheet (see Fig. A.3).
4 When a satisfactory form has been developed and drawn up have sufficient copies printed/duplicated. It may be advisable/necessary for the designers to produce a draft form after completing other studies (questionnaires, interviews, observations, etc.) and discussing it with the client and users before it is finalised.
5 Determine how these forms are to be completed and by whom. Forms may, for example, be attached to a questionnaire to be completed by users and the client, and finally evaluated by the designers.

g. Brainstorming

This is an extremely fast and versatile group technique which may be used at all stages of the briefing and design process to generate a large variety of ideas and/or information (sources of information, questions for interviews, etc.).

1 State problem clearly and simply.
2 Select a group of people – small groups of between four and 12 people generally work best – to participate. Group members should ideally have some relevant knowledge/experience. No previous experience of brainstorming is necessary.

Space Requirements for: (Project name/job number etc)		Department: Space name/number:	
Function of space and activities Main: Secondary:		Number of occupants/users Max: Average: Types:	No of similar rooms required:
Access and relationship to other spaces Main: Secondary:		Floor area:	Ceiling height:

Furniture and equipment		Finishes	Services	Environmental	Other
Desk		Floor:	Plumbing:	Heating, ventilation and air-conditioning:	Doors:
Counter					
Table			Electrical:		
Chairs					Windows:
Bulletin board		Walls:			
Bookshelves				Lighting:	
Storage cupboards			Fire:		Colours:
Typewriter		Ceiling:			
VDU			Communications:	Acoustics:	Storage:
Duplicating equipment					
Switchboard					

Fig. A.3 *Example of standardised form for collecting room requirements of a new building. In this case a section of the form has been organised as a checklist. In certain circumstances the whole form may best be compiled in this way.*

3 Select a chairman/group leader who will be able to control the session, keep the pace going and encourage a relaxed, creative atmosphere. Someone may be required to record verbal responses.

4 Decide on a time-limit for the session which should not continue for too long – between 30 and 60 minutes seems to produce the best results.

5 The following should be made clear to the participants:
— There must be no criticism or analysis of ideas.
— As many ideas as possible must be generated within the predetermined time period: the more ideas there are the more chance there is of finding some that are really useful.
— They must not worry about ideas being practical or not: responses must be spontaneous and uninhibited.
— They should feel free to combine or build on the other ideas put forward.

6 Decide on method of recording spoken ideas, for example, on a blackboard or large roll of paper. An alternative method is to allow a preliminary period for participants to write their initial ideas down, and each then reads an idea in turn. Further ideas are written on separate cards as the session proceeds.

7 Sort out ideas into groups and evaluate them. The ideas themselves may not be the most valuable output: the different groups (or categories) may be used to expose a range of possible solution areas from which a serious search for a final answer can start.

h. Interaction matrix

A frequently used and most useful method for determining and/or visualising the patterns of interactions or relationships between a number of elements in a problem, for example, the connections/adjacencies required between the spaces/rooms in a building.

A matrix, in its most basic form, is a simple two-way grid on which all possible combinations, by pairs, of the elements are recorded and ranked. The matrix itself does not determine the interactions – it is rather a framework within which the information is set out and which assists the search for relationships (space, activity, organisational, functional, etc.) within a set of several elements.

1 Define the terms element and interaction/relationship as they apply to the specific problem, for example, room/space and adjacency/proximity.

2 Decide what, if any, form of ranking (scale of preference/priority) is to be applied, for example, in the case of adjacency of rooms the following scale may be used: 0 = not necessary, 1 = desirable or some, 2 = essential.

3 Draw up a matrix which sets out the complete range of possible interactions between every pair of elements and check for each pair whether or not interaction occurs (see Fig. A.4).

4 It is often not necessary to use both halves of a matrix, for example, when determining required adjacency between rooms – unless the direction of door swings is to be determined – and a so-called half-matrix may be used (see Fig. A.5).

5 Try to keep the number of elements to a maximum of 20 or 25 – in a very large project it is usually possible to group the elements in sub-sets. It can be difficult to complete all the judgements involved when a matrix contains large numbers of elements, and the possibility of errors is greatly increased.

A.

	A	B	C	D	E
A			●	●	
B					
C	●			●	
D	●		●		●
E				●	
	2	0	2	3	1

Fig. A.4 *In matrix (A) relationships between pairs of activities are simply marked in the grid: no ranking is used. The totals at the foot of the vertical columns give the number of relationships, and thus the importance of each element. In example (B) a closeness ranking is indicated in one half of the grid (E = especially important, I = important, O = average satisfies, U = unimportant and X = undesirable) and the reason governing this is indicated in the other half (1 = use of typing pool, 2 = noise, 3 = number of visitors, 4 = movement of paper, 5 = use of supplies).*

B.

	President	Purchasing	General sales and administration	Accounting	Production planning	Data processing	Mail and supply room	Reception
President		U	I	U	U	X	U	E
Purchasing			U	O	U	U	U	E
General sales and administration	1			I	O	E	I	I
Accounting		4	4		U	E	O	U
Production planning			4			I	U	U
Data processing	2		4	4	4		U	U
Mail and supply room			5	5				U
Reception	3	3	3					

Fig. A.5 *Matrix illustrating journeys between rooms by people working in a typical existing operating theatre suite. This can be used to decide what modifications are needed to reduce movement to a minimum and to combine the units in the most satisfactory way from all known points of view. (From* The Architects' Journal, *17 June 1964, p.1375).*

Total Journeys

Total Journeys	No.	Room
117	1	Sisters' changing room
171	2	Nurses' changing room
717	3	Surgeons' rest room
399	4	Surgeons' changing room
46	5	Superintendent's room
24	6	Medical store
395	7	Small theatre
376	8	Anaesthetic room no 1
711	9	Theatre room no 1
528	10	Sink room
488	11	Sterilising room
677	12	Scrub up room
1115	13	Ante-space and nurses' station
711	14	Theatre room no 2
376	15	Anaesthetic room no 2
395	16	Emergency theatre
254	17	Workroom and clean supply
146	18	Sterile supply room
249	19	Male staff changing room
546	20	Nurses' station
305	21	The entrance

i. Correlation diagrams

There are a variety of techniques (interaction nets, bubble and block diagrams, flow diagrams, etc.) which are used for displaying spatial or other relationships between elements within a design problem. Such diagrams are widely used as an intermediate step for generating the actual plan layout of a building, and for visualising all the factors and variables that have a bearing on the design process.

1 Collect and analyse data. It is generally advisable to use an interaction matrix to determine relationships/interactions.

2 In the case of the interaction net technique a preliminary diagram is drawn with elements (for example, functions or spaces) represented by symbols and arranged in a circle. Relationships/interactions are indicated by linking elements with lines which may be varied in weight (thickness) to show the relative importance of the connections. The diagram is then adjusted with elements rearranged to minimise the crossing of lines (considering the essential links first and, once these have been sorted out, the secondary ones) and to clarify the pattern of interaction looking for strong sub-groupings or clusters of elements (see Fig. A.6).

3 Bubble diagrams are usually sketched freehand with bubbles (representing elements drawn within each other, overlapping or separated by a link (line) depending on the relationships and connections. Lines can be used to indicate the distance between elements, the pattern of movement between elements, and/or the importance of the connection between each of them (see Fig. A.7).

4 Block diagrams, which are similar to bubble diagrams, consist of squares or rectangles – representing each space – that are drawn to scale (proportionally sized to the amount of floor area required). Each of the blocks can be cut out of paper or cardboard and shuffled around to test various arrangements.

5 A form of flow chart can be used to visualise or externalise all the factors and variables having a bearing on a particular design project. A roll of newsprint or brown paper attached to a wall can be used for this purpose. One approach is to:

   a draw up a classification of the main sub-components (elements) which are to be investigated (activites, materials, etc.);

   b list all the points that can be thought of, putting each under the classification that seems to make most sense;

   c establish relationships. By studying the chart connections may be found where none seemed to exist before. For example, in preparing a chart for a children's playground the list under activities may include climbing, running, sliding, jumping; under the heading of materials one may have listed heavy canvas, which, when stretched and supported is buoyant and comparatively resilient. Thus, a link may be established between this and 'jumping', suggesting a trampoline-like structure;

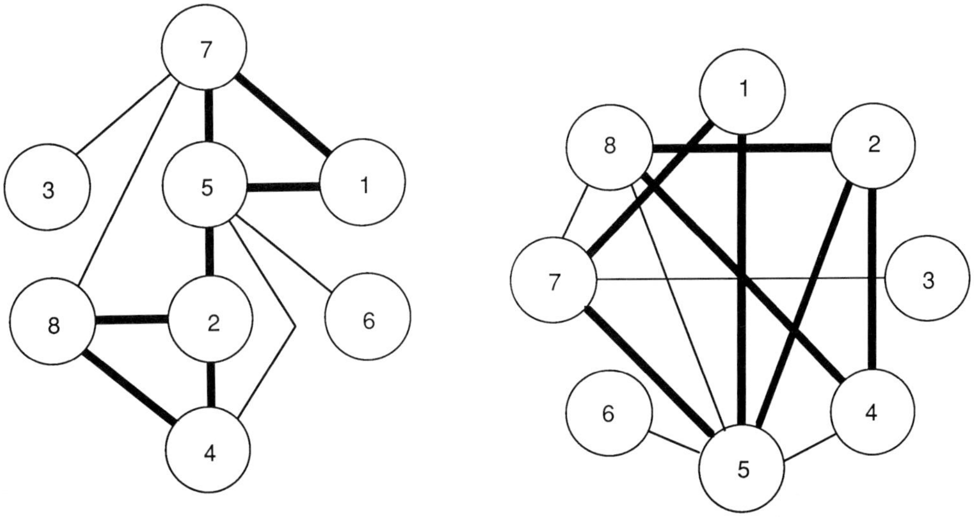

Fig. A.6 *The two basic stages of an interaction net illustrated very simply.*

Fig. A.7 *Bubble diagram used as a first step for generating actual plan layout of a building.*

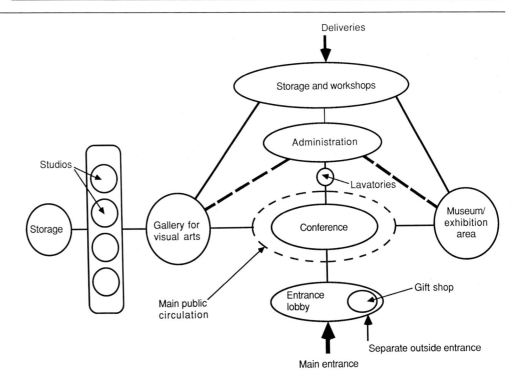

d   draw lines to connect relationships and possible things to do as a result of the connections (for example, design a trampoline-like structure), as they are established. New concepts, categories, relationships and solutions/things to do are filled-in as they come to mind during the briefing/design process; then

e   once this part of the chart has been more or less fully developed (it will never be complete) a second half consisting of implementation (who does what, when and how) can be added. The chart remains on the wall, being altered and amended until the work has been completed.

j.   Pattern language

This is a method developed by Christopher Alexander and his associates at the Centre for Environmental Structure at Berkeley, California, which is, theoretically, supposed to allow everyone to design for themselves the places they live and work in, while simultaneously giving order to the whole environment. The language consists of a 'dictionary' containing a set of patterns each of which suggests how a specific problem, which happens over and over again in an environment or a building, can be solved (see Fig. A.8). By selecting relevant patterns from Alexander's dictionary, generating others to suit local culture and conditions, and then combining them according to the specific needs of the project in question, a design can be created.

Although it may be naive to believe that the complex buildings and environments of today's industrialised society can be designed by users working with pattern books and without the aid of professional designers, there is a great deal of value in Alexander's work. For the purposes of education, the generation of ideas, the development of awareness, and involvement during the briefing and design process, Alexander's book of patterns can be an invaluable tool not only for designers but also for clients and users.

k. Cost planning

The object of cost planning (see Fig. A.9) (usually the responsibility of the appointed quantity surveyor) is to ensure that the final cost of a building project does not exceed the client's original budget figure.

A start should be made on analysing and controlling costs as early as possible in the briefing and design process. This will avoid the costly and time-consuming changes that result when it is discovered that costs exceed the budget *after* a design has been prepared.

1 Establish cost limitations at the start of the project: the client often stipulates a limit in his initial statement (preliminary brief).

2 Prepare a realistic preliminary estimate as early as possible (usually during the feasibility phase) either to confirm that the cost limitation is realistic in terms of the stated requirements, or to enable those involved to begin the inevitable trade-offs.

3 The preliminary estimate must often be based on the requirements defined during the development of the brief:

— Space: the floor area required.

— The use to which the space will be put.

— Quality: the standard of finishes, fittings and equipment required.

— External works.

— The maintenance and running costs the client is prepared to meet.

The estimate is generally calculated by using a cost per m^2 of floor area, based on an analysis of costs of the same, or similar, requirements in actual construction of a particular building type. Other techniques, for example, unit method in certain building types, may be used. The figure will be adjusted to suit local conditions and to take inflation into account. Included in the estimate will be all, or some, of the following:

— professional fees;

— administration and other expenses of the client (for example, legal fees);

— cost of the site and/or demolition;

— finance (mortgages, etc.); and

— risk and profit element (for example, if the building has to provide an economic return).

It is not an easy task for the quantity surveyor to prepare a realistic estimate as, amongst other things, much depends on his ability to detect the degree of

Fig. A.8 *The main points of three patterns, adapted from* A Pattern Language.

Positive outdoor space
Outdoor spaces which are merely 'left over' between buildings will, in general, not be used.

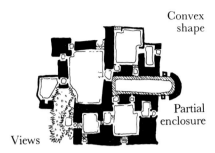

Convex shape

Partial enclosure

A. Buildings that create negative, leftover space.

B. Buildings that create positive outdoor space.

Views

Therefore:

Make all the outdoor spaces which surround and lie between your buildings positive. Give each one some degree of enclosure; surround each space with wings of buildings, trees, hedges, fences, arcades, and trellised walks, until it becomes an entity with positive quality and does not spill out indefinitely around corners.

Cascade of roofs
Few buildings will be structurally and socially intact, unless the floors step down towards the end of the wings, and unless the roof, accordingly, forms a cascade.

Social entities   Corresponding roofs

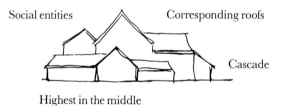

Cascade

Highest in the middle

Therefore:

Visualize the whole building, or building complex, as a system of roofs. Place the largest, highest, and widest roofs over those parts of the building which are most significant; when you come to lay the roofs out in detail, you will be able to make all lesser roofs cascade off these large roofs and form a stable self-buttressing system, which is congruent with the hierarchy of social spaces underneath the roofs.

Intimacy gradient
Unless the spaces in a building are arranged in a sequence which corresponds to their degree of privateness, the visits made by strangers, friends, guests, clients, family, will always be a little awkward.

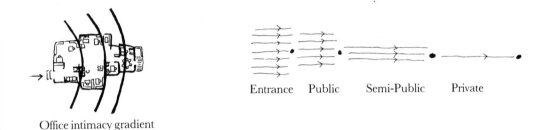

Entrance   Public   Semi-Public   Private

Office intimacy gradient

Therefore:

Lay out the spaces of the building so that they create a sequence which begins with the entrance and the most public parts of the building, then leads into the slightly more private areas, and finally to the most private domains.

buildability in the designer's proposals. A more detailed estimate is prepared once there is a final scheme design to work from.

— As work proceeds the quantity surveyor will prepare cost studies of alternative solutions, test economic viability, and check regularly that requirements and proposals will not result in expenses that are likely to exceed the cost limit.

— Once a realistic estimate is agreed a cost plan is generally prepared. This plan establishes how the approved estimate will be spent by allocating parts of the sum to individual elements: roof, external walls, wall finishes, heating installation etc (see Fig. A.10). Costs are allocated on a quality basis, usually related to an analysis of completed buildings rather than to specification decisions made for the project in question (these usually happen later in the process). The plan is not a design straightjacket but a framework influencing decision-making and within which the detailed design and specification must be developed. Adjustments can be made as the work proceeds but must be done systematically and under control, so that additional expenditure on one element is balanced by savings on others.

— There are various methods of cost evaluation (not described here), such as life-cycle cost analysis, value analysis and cost-benefit analysis, that may be used to assist in making briefing and design decisions.

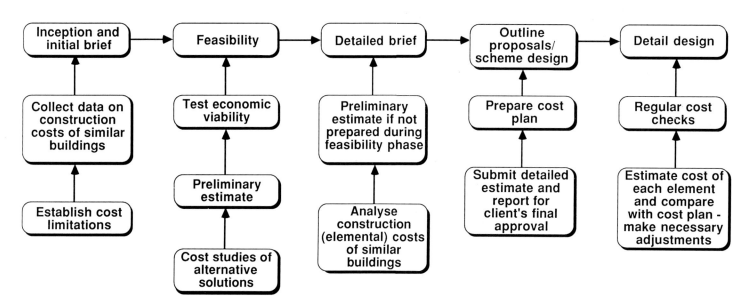

Fig. A.9 *Chart indicating basic cost planning procedures in relation to the main briefing and design phases.*

Summary of element costs

Fig. A.10. *Example of summary element costs for two sports centres constructed in the UK 1978-81. (Taken from building studies published in* The Architects' Journal, *24 March 1982: Bury St Edmunds Sports Centre; 2 September 1981: Elswick Park Pool, Newcastle-upon-Tyne.)*

	Bury St Edmunds Sports Centre		Elswick Park Pool, Newcastle-upon-Tyne	
	Cost per m^2 (£)	Per cent of total	Cost per m^2 (£)	Per cent of total
Preliminaries and insurances	9.75	3.15	25.34	5.53
Contingencies	4.17	1.35	7.14	1.56
Work below lowest floor finish	0.52	0.17	64.27	14.05
Structural elements				
Frame	41.88	13.54	31.84	6.96
Upper floors	1.23	0.40	5.08	1.11
Roof	20.25	6.54	29.82	6.51
Rooflights	0.06	0.02	31.84	6.96
Staircases	3.03	0.98	0.96	0.21
External walls	31.06	10.04	25.97	5.67
External doors	0.37	0.12	3.43	0.75
Partitions	17.54	5.67	19.09	4.17
Internal doors	2.92	0.94	3.59	0.78
Ironmongery	2.72	0.88	2.22	0.48
Total of structural elements	121.06	39.13	153.84	33.60
Finishes and fittings				
Wall finishes	10.31	3.33	17.02	3.72
Floor finishes	19.93	6.44	24.19	5.28
Ceiling finishes	22.10	7.14	15.12	3.30
Decoration	7.24	2.34	3.69	0.81
Fittings	7.24	2.34	17.69	3.86
Total of finishes and fittings	66.82	21.59	77.71	16.97
Services				
Sanitary appliances	1.21	0.39	1.73	0.38
Waste, soil and overflow pipes	0.96	0.31	0.30	0.07
Cold and hot water services	4.07	1.32	4.57	1.00
Heating and ventilation services	57.29	18.51	45.15	9.87
Electrical services	38.43	12.42	31.67	6.92
Special services	4.98	1.61	41.53	9.08
Drainage	0.14	0.05	4.43	0.97
Total of services	107.08	34.61	129.38	28.29
Total	309.40	100.00	457.68	100.00
External works	£11,912		£285,357	

Summary:

Bury St Edmunds Sports Centre
Ground floor area: 2483 m^2
Total floor area: 4272 m^2
Type of contract: JCT Local Authorities Edition with Approximate Quantities 1975
Tender date: 1 July 1980
Work began: 4 August 1980
Work finished: 11 September 1981
Price of foundation, superstructure, installation and finishes including drainage to collecting manhole: £1,321,778
Price of external works and ancillary buildings including drainage beyond collecting manhole: £11,912   Total: £1,333,690

Summary:

Elswick Park Pool, Newcastle-upon-Tyne
Ground floor area: 1699 m^2
Total floor area: 2178 m^2
Type of contract: fluctuating (31F) JCT with quantities
Tender date: 21 September 1978
Work began: 16 October 1978
Work finished: 21 January 1981
Price of foundation, superstructure, installation and finishes including drainage to collecting manhole: £996,827
Price of external works and ancillary buildings including drainage beyond collecting manhole: £285,357   Total: £1,282,184

Conversion Factors and Tables

The system of measures used in this book is 'Système International d'Unités' known in all languages as SI units which are based on the following:

Quantity	Name of unit	Unit symbol
Length	metre	m
Mass	kilogram	kg
Time	second	s
Electric current	ampere	A
Thermodynamic temperature	kelvin*	k
Luminous intensity	candela	cd

* The degree Celsius (°C) is used for all practical purposes.

Quantity	Conversion factors	
Length	1.0 mm	= 0.039 in
	25.4 mm (2.54 cm)	= 1 in
	304.8 mm (30.48 cm)	= 1 ft
	914.4 mm	= 1 yd
	1 000.0 mm (1.0 m)	= 1 yd 3.4 in (1.093 yd)
	20.117 m	= 1 chain
	1 000.00 m (1 km)	= 0.621 mile
	1 609.31 m	= 1 mile

Area	100 mm^2 (1.0 cm^2)	= 0.155 in^2
	645.2 mm^2 (6.452 cm^2)	= 1 in^2
	929.03 cm^2 (0.093 m^2)	= 1 ft^2
	0.836 m^2	= 1 yd^2
	1.0 m^2	= 1.196 yd^2 (10.763 ft^2)
	0.405 ha (4046.9 m^2)	= 1 acre
	1.0 ha (10 000 m^2)	= 2.471 acre
	1.0 km^2	= 0.386 mile^2
	2.59 km^2 (259 ha)	= 1 mile^2

Temperature	X°C	= ($\frac{9}{5}$X + 32) °F
	$\frac{5}{9}$ × (X − 32) °C	= X°F

Illumination	1 lx (1 lumen/m^2)	= 0.093 ft-candle (0.093 lumen/ft^2)
	10.764 lx	= 1.0 ft-candle (1 lumen/ft^2)

Mass	1.0 g	= 0.035 oz (avoirdupois)
	28.35 g	= 1 oz (avoirdupois)
	454.0 g (0.454 kg)	= 1 lb
	1 000.0 g (1 kg)	= 2.205 lb
	45.36 kg	= 1 cwt US
	907.2 kg (0.907 t)	= 1 ton US
	1 000.0 kg (1.0 t)	= 1.102 ton US

Force	1.0 N	= 0.225 lbf
	1.0 kgf (9.807 N; 1.0 kilopond)	= 2.205 lbf
	4.448 kN	= 1.0 kipf (1 000 lbf)
	8.897 kN	= 1.0 tonf US

Force per unit length	1.0 N/m	= 0.067 lbf/ft
	14.59 N/m	= 1.0 lbf/ft
	175.1 kN/m (175.1 N/mm)	= 1.0 lbf/ft

Tables

Length

mm ⟷ in

mm	in	mm	in
25.4 1	0.04	254.0 10	0.39
50.8 2	0.08	508.0 20	0.79
76.2 3	0.12	762.0 30	1.18
101.6 4	0.16	1016.0 40	1.57
127.0 5	0.2	1270.0 50	1.97
152.4 6	0.24	1524.0 60	2.36
177.8 7	0.28	1778.0 70	2.76
203.2 8	0.31	2032.0 80	3.15
228.6 9	0.35	2286.0 90	3.54
		2540.0 100	3.93

m ⟷ ft

m	ft	m	ft
0.3 1	3.28	3.05 10	32.8
0.61 2	6.56	6.1 20	65.62
0.91 3	9.84	9.14 30	98.43
1.22 4	13.12	12.19 40	131.23
1.52 5	16.4	15.24 50	164.04
1.83 6	19.69	18.29 60	196.85
2.13 7	22.97	21.34 70	229.66
2.44 8	26.25	24.38 80	262.47
2.74 9	29.53	27.43 90	295.28
		30.48 100	328.08

Area

m^2 ⟷ ft^2

m^2	ft^2	m^2	ft^2
0.093 1	10.76	0.93 10	107.64
0.19 2	21.53	1.86 20	215.28
0.28 3	32.29	2.79 30	322.92
0.37 4	43.06	3.72 40	430.56
0.46 5	53.82	4.65 50	538.2
0.56 6	64.58	5.57 60	645.84
0.65 7	75.35	6.5 70	753.47
0.74 8	86.11	7.43 80	861.11
0.84 9	96.88	8.36 90	968.75
		9.29 100	1076.39

Volume

m^3 ⟷ ft^3

m^3	ft^3	m^3	ft^3
0.03 1	35.32	0.28 10	353.15
0.06 2	70.63	0.57 20	706.29
0.08 3	105.94	0.85 30	1059.44
0.11 4	141.26	1.13 40	1412.59
0.14 5	176.57	1.42 50	1765.73
0.17 6	211.89	1.7 60	2118.88
0.2 7	247.2	1.98 70	2472.03
0.23 8	282.52	2.27 80	2825.17
0.25 9	317.83	2.55 90	3178.32
		2.83 100	3531.47